On the Principles of Taxing Beer

On the Principles of Taxing Beer

And Other Brief Philosophical Essays

James V. Schall

ST. AUGUSTINE'S PRESS
South Bend, Indiana

Manufactured in the United States of America.

1 2 3 4 5 6   25 24 23 22 21 20 19

Library of Congress Cataloging in Publication Data
Schall, James V., author.
[Essays. Selections]
On the principles of taxing beer : and other brief philosophical essays /
by James V. Schall.
pages cm
ISBN 978-1-58731-615-9 (hardback)
1. Philosophy. I. Title.
BD41.S265 2015
191--dc23   2015032107

∞ The paper used in this publication meets the minimum requirements of the American National Standard for Information Sciences - Permanence of Paper for Printed Materials, ANSI Z39.48-1984.

St. Augustine's Press
www.staugustine.net

"Socrates: 'It really is a disgrace to the soul in each of us that it plainly doesn't know what in it constitutes goodness and badness for it, whereas what constitutes goodness and badness for the body, and other things, is something it has already considered.'"
—Plato, *Meno*, 321d.

"'Many are the strange chances of the world,' said Mithrandir, 'and help shall oft come from the hands of the weak when the Wise falter."
—J. R. R. Tolkien, "Of the Rings of Power and the Third Age."

"Happy the man who meditates on wisdom, and reflects on knowledge; who ponders her ways in his heart, and understands her paths...."
—Sirach, 15, 20–21.

"Of course, the real objection which a philosophical Christian would bring against the religion of Omar is not that he gives no place to God, it is that he gives too much place to God. His is the terrible theism which can imagine nothing else but deity, and which denies altogether the outlines of human personality and will."
—G. K. Chesterton, "Omar and the Sacred Vine," *Heretics*.

"There are some who...both themselves assert that it is possible for the same thing to be and not to be, and say that people can judge this to be the case. And among others, many writers about nature use this language. But...it is impossible for anything at the same time to be and not to be, and by this means to have shown that this is the most indisputable of all principles. –Some through want of education, for not to know of what things one should demand demonstration, and what one should not, argues want of education."
—Aristotle, *Metaphysics*, 1006a1–8.

"Still you've got one consolation." "What's that?" "'The thought that all that befalls you is part of the great web, ha, ha, ha,' said Gussie, and exited smiling."
—P. G. Wodehouse, *The Mating Season*, Chapter 9.

"The soul of man, formed for eternal life, naturally springs forward beyond the limits of corporeal existence, and rejoices to consider herself as co-operating with future ages and as co-existent with endless duration."

—Samuel Johnson, *The Rambler*, #49, Tuesday, 4 September 1750

ACKNOWLEDGEMENTS

I should like to thank Robert Royal at The Catholic Thing, Gerald Russello at the University Bookman, John Vella at Crisis Magazine and Inside Catholic, Dale Alquist at Gilbert Magazine, Gerald Gerson at the Catholic Pulse, Excelsis, and Joseph Pearce at the St. Austin Review for permission to republish the following Essays in their sites.

1) The Catholic Thing, Chapters 1, 7, 11. 13, 15, 17, 20, 21, 22, 23, 29, 31, 32, 33, 34, 36, 37, 38, 39, 40, 42, 43, 44, 45, 46, 49, 50, 51, 53, 55, 56, 57

2) Crisis Magazine: Chapters 2, 4, 5, 12, 14, 18, 19, 24, 27, 48, 52

3) Gilbert Magazine: 25, 41

4) Catholic Pulse: Chapter 8

5) Excelsis, (No longer in print): Chapter 9

6) University Bookman: Chapters 3, 10, 30, 47, 54, 58, 59

7) St. Austin Review: Chapters 3, 35

TABLE OF CONTENTS

A Brief Foreword

Much can be said for long Russian novels and extensive German treatises, even multi-volume ones. Yet, the human mind is often desirous of brevity. "Explain this issue to me in a few words" is an oft-heard request. Aphorisms and maxims have their place, as writers from the Book of Proverbs, to the Roman Martial, and on to Nietzsche have shown us. One cannot exactly say that the short essay lies somewhere between the length of *War and Peace* and a succinct epigram. And some things, like Aquinas' writings, are coherent, organized collections of short concise "articles." Josef Pieper compares the brevity of Aquinas' "articles," in which he presents his argument, with the classic "essay" that is not so tightly argued.

The essay can range over a wide number of things. And, as I note here, it can be "philosophic" too. In a lovely passage in his *Guide to Thomas Aquinas*, Pieper writes: "To philosophize means...to concentrate our gaze on the totality of encountered phenomena and methodologically to investigate the coherency of them all and the meaning of the Whole..." (147). The "concentration of our gaze" on a particular something in this world—it matters not what—is the context of the essay. An essay can be about anything—as we see here, from "taxing beer" to reading Lord Peter Wimsey and P. G. Wodehouse, to wondering about whether the universe is "empty." And it is true, as the very notion of *what is*, of being itself, can lead us to the "Whole," as Pieper called it.

Each of my previous collections of essays—*Idylls & Rambles, Schall on Chesterton, Meditations Late in the XXth Century, Remembering Belloc, Another Sort of Learning, The Praise of "Sons of Bitches,"* and *The Classical Moment*—has something to do with Belloc as an essayist. His essays are simply the best of their kind. I have to laugh when I read the names of some of Belloc's collections of essays—*On Everything* (1909), *On Anything* (1910), *On Something* (1910, *On Nothing and Kindred Subjects* (2005), and in 1922 simply *On*. So the reader will not be surprised to find each of the essays in this book begins with the great preposition "On." This is the classic way to introduce any essay.

As to the number of items to be included in a collection of "selected essays," there is no rule, certainly not six, certainly not one hundred and forty-three. The Penguin edition of Belloc's *Selected Essays* contains 42 essays, while J. B. Morton's *Selected Essays* from Methuen contains 54 essays. Thus, somewhere in the late fifties seems like a good place to stop. Most of these essays are "brief," short, some eight hundred words or so. A few will have eleven or twelve hundred words. In general, there is a certain lightsomeness to these essays. I am a believer in Chesterton's remark that just because a topic is serious or profound, is still no reason why it cannot, at the same time, be funny or amusing.

I am in the general habit of introducing books of mine with a series of citations from various authors. The seven citations of this book should be read, if it strikes one's fancy, before turning to the subsequent essays. The essays here touch on one or other of these great themes that form our mind and our kind. Philosophical essays are, in essence, designed to enable us to think and think clearly. The very purpose of thinking is to know the truth as found in things, to know *what is*. Let me say a word about each of them.

The first citation from Plato's *Meno* suggests that the purpose of our soul, with its intellectual faculties, is to arrive at the truth that there is indeed a difference between "goodness and badness." Plato suggests that the failure to arrive at the fact of such a distinction is not because there is some confusion in *what is*, in reality. Rather the problem lies in our willingness to live according to the distinction.

The second citation is from an Appendix containing the cited essay. I found it in a Taiwan edition of the *Silmarillion*. A friend of mine located it in a used book store on Turk Street in San Francisco. This reflection is the great theme from the Nativity, that the great things of the world do not necessarily occur only with the great and well-known. Many of the greatest things are in a weakness that is still able to see and act on what is to be done.

The third passage is from the Book of Sirach in the Old Testament. Wisdom is what most easily relates Hebrew thought to Greek thought. Aristotle had said that the beginning of wisdom was wonder. In the Old Testament, the beginning is the fear of the Lord that brings us to wisdom. All men, Aristotle tells us, seek happiness in all their actions. In the Book of Sirach, the man is "happy" who meditates, reflects, ponders, and understands wisdom's "paths."

The fourth citation takes up Chesterton's awareness of the importance of ideas and distinctions. In these days of Muslim rebirth, Chesterton seems already to have touched on the roots of Muslim thought in voluntarism. Omar was a Sufi who taught Avicenna's philosophy. In Islam, philosophy came to attribute all secondary causality to Allah. In this sense, it evaporates any activity on the part of finite beings. Chesterton calls it a "terrible deity" that can imagine nothing but the deity.

The whole point of Genesis and of Aristotle, for that matter, was that there really are other things besides Allah and these things really act. The prohibition of drink of the "vine" is an implicit denial of the goodness of things. Actions of men and things are not illusions. God is not praised by denying the actions of things other than God.

The fifth selection is from Aristotle's *Metaphysics*. This is the classic passage that establishes first principles of being and thought. If we insist on "proving" everything, we will regress to infinity. The first principle, that of non-contradiction, is the basis of all being and all thought. Aristotle simply tells us that our inability to understand this truth or to admit it is what is meant by a lack of education. It is, indeed, "impossible for anything at the same time to be and not to be." If we do not begin there, we cannot begin at all.

The sixth is a snippet from a Bertie Wooster novel of P. G. Wodehouse. If we examine the passage, we are suddenly before the issue of Providence, of how things that go wrong can fit together with things that go right. Wodehouse refers to this issue as the "great web" of being. This notion has Stoic and modern ecological overtones of determinism. But the passage is ironic. Gussie Fink-Nottle exits "smiling," as if to say that Bertie's "one consolation" is that, in the end, things will be all right. This is good philosophy, not simply naiveté. It is aware that things can also go wrong.

The final citation is from Samuel Johnson. He taught us all about the essay, about living a full life. An analogy is at work here. Johnson tells us that we are made for "eternal life." Socrates held that our souls are immortal. We transcend in our mind, without denying it, the particularity of things. The fact that our thoughts are universal does not only lead us to direct our lives to our ultimate end. It also, sometimes dangerously, directs us to our inner-worldly future and its enterprises.

The essence of "modernity," as I argued in *The Modern Age*, is to transpose our supernatural end into a natural one in this age. Johnson hints at why this confusion is possible. We do look beyond our own corporeal existence into the lives of our posterity and to the "endless duration" of life on this earth. Benedict XVI referred to this issue in *Spe Solvi*. But this awareness of "eternal life," as Johnson intimated, opens us both to what went before us and to what will happen beyond our own limited days. Since the origin of the "great web" and of "eternal life" is related through the being of man, we can be content that the one does not contradict the other.

These essays are, as I mentioned, each "brief." The little longer, "On Travel," refers to an essay of that same title by Francis Bacon. He is considered, with Montaigne, to be the modern founder of the essay. We cannot forget that Seneca and Horace, among the Romans, likewise used this delightful form. And I call these essays "philosophical." Beginning from *what is*, they lead to the Whole. On the way, they pass by Belloc's "everything," "anything," "something," and "nothing." In short, they are "ON" any fact in this world, with its seemingly "endless duration."

But we know with our minds that a thing cannot be and not be at the same time. We also know universals, both man and Socrates. We know what is also revealed. We can think of "the end of all things," of "end times," and of "luck." These considerations also pertain to the Whole to which all philosophy is directed once it begins in the *what is* that first incited the mind to know, not nothing, but any existing thing at all.

These essays do not follow any particular order. They are written in different times and in different places. Yet, they are all by the same person. They relate to a similar mood, a similar habit of mind. We begin in *what is*. We are not content simply to stay there after we "gaze" on any existing thing long enough to suspect that nothing we directly encounter fully explains itself. Whether we begin with a tax on beer, the execution of Mary, Queen of Scots, envy, the tyrant, Screwtape's "hairy biped," the origins of the Qur'an, pleasures, evil, Bertie Wooster, Charles Schulz, or the "empty universe," we are led on to the Whole. This Whole is the proper object of wonder, of the mind. Whether even this inner-worldly "Whole" explains itself is itself doubtful.

In the beginning, there was "nothing." The world *that is* need not exist, nor do we individually "need" to exist within it. Briefly stated, something cannot come from nothingness. Revelation begins, not with "In the beginning there was 'nothing'," but with "In the beginning was the Word, the *Logos*." These essays circle around *what is* and what is not. They reflect the truth that *what is* does not originate in what is not. This realization is why I included in this collection Chapter 4, "On *the Lord of the World*" and Chapter 33, "On *The City of God*." With due apologies to Omar and the Vine, and in hope of low taxes on the common man's ordinary beverage, these essays may or may not become clearer with a good beer. But surely they will become more pleasant in light of the Whole, of the Great Web of being, of what stands outside of nothingness.

Chapter 1

ON THE END OF ALL THINGS

Before anything begins, God *is*. That is, God stands outside of nothingness. God is all-complete, existing with an inner Trinitarian life that needs no world, no man, and no angel. If anything but God exists, it is not because something is deficient or lonely in God. What is not God cannot explain itself to itself without God. *God's purpose in creation is to associate other knowing beings, angels and men, in His inner life.* This purpose never changes.

No "natural" angelic or human condition ever in fact existed, even though it might have. That is, both angels and men were, from the beginning, intended to be more than their nature allowed them to expect by their own good but limited being. "*Homo non proprie humanus sed superhumanus est.*" ("Properly speaking, man is not a natural but a supernatural being"). This "elevated" condition, however, was not "due" to man or angel, but was given to them in order that the primary end of creation be realized.

The cosmos finds its purpose through its relation to the initial design of God in inviting rational beings to His inner, Trinitarian life. Even though the cosmos comes first in time, it does not come first in the divine intention. God could not simply associate free beings with Himself apart from their free being. As Plato said in the *Symposium*, moreover, the universe seemed to need, for its own perfection, free creatures, who could appreciate it. The free creature can reject that for which it exists.

The Fall is the account of free creatures claiming themselves to be the cause of the order and nature of things. The essential temptation is for oneself, not God, to be the cause of the distinction between good and evil. God's only choice, to avoid this unpleasant possibility, would be not to create at all, so that nothing but God would exist. As such, this would not be a bad thing. God would commit no evil in not creating. Yet, something in the goodness of God seeks to diffuse itself not of necessity but of delight. This aspect of goodness is what lies at the origin of our being and that of creation.

Evidently, from the beginning, the First Parents, like the angels, were themselves intended for the initial purpose of God in creation. They were not simply "natural" human beings. Had they definitively not sinned, their destiny would have been the elevated relation to the inner life of God that is promised to all rational creation. We do not know how this would have worked. What changed with the Fall was not the ultimate end for which human beings were created, but rather the means whereby, granted the free rejection of God's initial plan, this end could be achieved.

Through the Promises to Israel and the Incarnation and through both to all the nations, revelation did not change the end for which God created in the first place. It did change the means by which that purpose was to be achieved. Man would be saved, as even the Greeks suspected, by suffering. The Incarnation and Redemption restored to man a definite way of reaching the original end for which he was created. The Redemption did not, however, restore the elevated gifts, especially that gift of not dying, that was given to the original human free beings.

Of course, God understood that the Fall would happen, but His knowing did not cause it to happen. The cause lies in the will and love of the free creature. The Incarnation and Redemption, the Cross and Resurrection, are the way that human beings are to return to God's initial purpose. The *"felix culpa"* does imply that the Incarnation, in the way we know it, is the surprising, almost shocking response of God to our freedom. We would like, perhaps, to think of some "gentler" way. But the particular Incarnation and Redemption that we know in revelation, teach us both the terrible consequences of sin and the extraordinary free glory into which we are invited in God's initial purpose.

The original plan of God in creation is being worked out in history. Our unique lives are immersed in this very working out. The most important thing in history is that we achieve the end for which we are created. This end is offered to everyone. As John Paul II often said, God does not deny the means for those of good will who seek.

But all of this possibility is dependent on the Incarnation and the Redemption through Church and sacrament that Christ has revealed to be the way back to our end. This end is to live eternal life beholding, delighting in the inner life of God in the company of all beings who choose to accept this end, an acceptance that no one can achieve without grace and personal choice.

Chapter 2
ON WHAT WE DON'T KNOW

A professor I once knew gave history tests in the following format: "Draw a line down the center of the page. On the left side, write what you know on the subject; on the right side, what you do not know." The logical temptation of such instruction is to put as many things possible on the left side and, on the right, a blank. How can someone be expected to write about what he does not know? The usual case is to write many things about what we do not know, but *think* we know. These are Socratic sounding questions. We should not claim to know what we do not know.

Yet, something fascinating hovers about what we do not know. In general, we may not know something in order to concentrate on what takes much time. We are content, for instance, not to know the interesting geography of Antarctica in order to figure out how to make a better gym shoe or even how to save our soul. The human mind is infinite in what it can know. What usually prevents us from knowing something, besides a certain dullness, is time or proper training.

What substitutes for what I do not actively know? Generally, it is authority. With regard to most of the truths that we actually live by, we accept them on authority. This is as true in matters of daily living as it is true of faith. What, after all, is a map or a blueprint on how to put a toy together but a statement of authority about how something is? The assumption is that the authority knows. Following authority is not the same as acting blindly or in ignorance. Thus, "what we don't know" does not necessarily paralyze us. We can act on authority to find that it generally works.

On Tuesday, April 18, 1775, Samuel Johnson was at a beautiful Thames villa owned by a certain Mr. Cambridge. Johnson, once in the spacious house library, made a quick run over the books. Johnson overheard Sir Joshua Reynolds, in a loud "aside," criticize him "for looking only at the backs of the books." Johnson, as Boswell put it, "ever ready for contest, instantly started from his reverie, wheeled about, and answered, 'Sir, the reason is very plain. Knowledge is of two kinds. We know a subject ourselves or we know where we can find information about it. When we inquire into any subject, the first thing we have to do is to know what books have treated of it. This leads us to look at catalogues, and the backs of books in libraries'" (I, 595). Even if we do not know something, we know where to go to find it. This is a precious intelligence. Writing down what we do not know on the right hand side of the exam may have a point after all!

To translate this examining "backs of books" into modern terms, someone recently asked me about "the Illuminati," about whom I knew little. I went to Google, The Illuminati were a secret 18th century society founded by a graduate of a Jesuit college. It figures.

During Christmas, visiting a nephew, I found an elegant edition of *Treasure Island*. If I read it before, I no longer recall it. I was charmed by it. The sailors on the *Hispaniola*, I read, were given "duff every other day." I wondered what this phrase meant. I do recall the colloquial expression "get off your duff." I remember asking my niece what it might mean. Maybe it meant that the sailors were given light duty every other day. But "getting off one's duff" usually meant work.

For Christmas, I was once given the *Merriam-Webster's Collegiate Dictionary*, 10th Edition. When I returned home, I went to the "backs of my reference books" to this dictionary. The second meaning of "duff" is indeed "buttocks." The expression "get off your..." is given as an example. The third meaning is something "worthless"—a British expression from around 1889.

The first meaning of "duff,." however, was, from 1816, an alternate to "dough." It means "a boiled or steamed pudding, often containing dried fruit." A second meaning was "partly decayed matter on a forest floor." A third meaning was "fine coal." When the sailors were given "duff" every other day, it simply meant that they were given pudding! My mind was at rest.

All of this proves Johnson's point about the vastness of what we don't know. We are curious beings. We can look at the "backs of books" until we find one that is likely to inform us. What we don't know is the beginning of an adventure to take us to what we do know, what we want to know.

Chapter 3
ON THE PRINCIPLES FOR TAXING BEER

In *G. K.'s Weekly* for November 19, 1932 (165), we find a very interesting essay by G. C. Heseltine entitled: "Is Beer a Luxury?" No doubt we often lie awake at night pondering this deep metaphysical question. This title recalls Chesterton's own quip: In response to those who claim that we drink beer because of the alcohol in it, he remarked that "Anyone who claims that we drink beer for this purpose (alcohol) has never walked thirstily down a dusty English road on a hot summer's day." Though it was written during the Depression and Prohibition in America, Heseltine was not initially provoked to write his essay so much by the teetotalers as by the tax-men.

In examining the bureaucratic mind, Heseltine noted that by defining beer as a "luxury" instead of as a "necessity," it would be possible in good conscience to place a much higher tax on beer than would be possible were it considered to be a food or drink or normal necessity. The government economist is interested in beer because he can steadily raise taxes on it, without too much notice, at least until the law of diminishing returns sets in when he begins to get less money for higher taxes. The prohibitionist, on the other hand, seeks a high tax in order to discourage any drinking at all.

Heseltine draws some fine distinctions. He admits that we can live without beer. But "it does not follow that because you can do without a thing, that it is not a necessity." Nor does it seem to be a virtue to abstain from something simply because you can do so "without apparent harm." If it is a virtue to abstain, we must look at our motive in doing so. To the teetotaler advocate, total abstinence from beer, at all times and places, is alone held (wrongly) to be a virtue, the virtue of self-control, moderation. But if you can persuade people that beer is also a "pure luxury," in addition to being a vice, then your case against drinking can be made more socially acceptable and easily.

In order to test the validity of such strained logic, Heseltine observed that some folks can also live without eating meat. Excessive meat-eating, however, also brings out some social evils. We already, in recent years, have the anti-obesity crowd who want to force us to give up anything that would give us extra weight—again often for reasons of taxation, to lessen the tax burden in paying for their health problems.

But Heseltine thinks that the problem is not with the beer itself or the meat or food. It arises from having too much of it, at the wrong time, the wrong place, and the wrong circumstances. He places the problem where it should be placed, on our self-rule. "There is hardly a single article of diet that some men cannot be found able to do without, or find a substitute for." The vast literature on diets proves this. If you would take all the recommended diets currently available and simply list what they said you could not eat; almost all human food would be excluded and definitely all human food worth eating for the pleasure of eating. Heseltine is quite amusing: "We know that most people, deprived of certain foods (such as those containing specific vitamins) will develop diseases, and that such deprivation, if universally applied, would exterminate or seriously damage the whole human race."

The fact that some men can abstain from certain foods and drinks does not mean that the things they abstain from are, for that reason, luxuries, or that we can or should do without them. Very many people could probably continue to live healthy lives if deprived, for instance, of meat. As civilization declines, vegetarians abound, probably because we think more of our bodies than of our souls.

No scientific body, Heseltine thinks, would recommend as a universal principle the not drinking of beer or wine for the whole human race. Why not? "Nobody knows what results might follow, physical as well as mental and social, if the human race were suddenly and totally deprived of beer and wine." Thus, we cannot say to what degree they may be necessary or unnecessary. Nor can we conclude, on this basis, that beer and wine are luxuries and not necessities.

Was Heseltine actually implying, back in 1932, that such drink may be a "necessity?" "When we find that mankind throughout its history, in almost every climate, civilization, and condition, has had certain habits and articles of diet in common, it would be a good deal more than rash to assume that such things are not in some way, though we may not know exactly how, essential and necessary to humanity." Again, anything can be abused by individuals, but the possibility of abuse ought not to become a universal principle for all. If it did, it would deprive us of the very notion of the virtue of temperance or moderation, as well as depriving us of something that is contributory to the abundance of life.

No doubt it is possible to live a solitary life, but most of us long for company. It is possible to eat grass and such vegetarian things, but most people, if they can find it or hunt it, enjoy a good pork chop or roasted chicken or a rabbit once in a while. "Though some men have lived on water, the history of mankind shows men are naturally drinkers of fermented drinks like beer and wine."

The Aristotelian position was that two extremes are found to every virtue, a too much and a too little. Heseltine argued for the middle ground, for the virtue, the not too much and the not too little. He saw no reason to think that because some abuse in eating meat or drinking beer was a vice, that the not eating meat or drinking beer at all was thereby automatically a virtue. "There is nothing...to justify the assumption that these common factors (that most people drink beer or eat meat) are not necessary, and that prohibiting or excessive restriction will not be harmful."

As to the tax experts and economists working for governments all over the world, they remain tempted to call beer and wine a luxury. That way they can raise the prices to a point of diminishing returns, to a point where, what is a normal and ordinary thing, indeed becomes a luxury. This proposal too, I think, is a sign of the decline of civilization.

Chapter 4
ON *THE LORD OF THE WORLD*

In 2001 (surely not on 9/11!), St. Augustine's Press published a new edition of Robert Hugh Benson's 1907 novel, *The Lord of the World*. A friend of mine in Vermont recently urged me to read it. I did.

Ralph McInerny, in a brief introduction, writes: "The novel wonderfully conveys the flatness and boredom of a world without God. Boredom becomes a condition for recognizing our need for something more than this—a few more decades of life and then a total void."

This novel is remarkably similar in theme to Benedict's Encyclical *Spe Salvi*, one of the very great encyclicals. That is, the novel is about the futility of a this-worldly utopia with the instruments of death (abortion, euthanasia) and endless death (prolongation of life, cloning) that are designed to make it come about. Indeed, in a lecture he gave at the Catholic University in Milan on February 6, 1992, Josef Ratzinger cited *The Lord of the World* and the deadly Universalist, inner-world atmosphere it depicted.

My father had this Benson novel around the house when I was a boy in Iowa. I remember reading it. What, at a young age, I remember most about it was how frightening it was to me with its vivid end-of-the world description. Indeed, I have often said that this novel and C. S. Lewis' *That Hideous Strength* are the most frightening books that I have ever read. Now, no longer a youth and then some, when I ask myself why this fright, it is because both books make a this-worldly triumph of evil seem so plausible, so intellectual, and so logical.

Both books seem to exemplify the validity of a remark of Herbert Deane in his book on Augustine: "As history draws to its close, the number of true Christians in the world will decline rather than increase. His (Augustine's) words give no support to the hope that the world will gradually be brought to belief in Christ and that earthly society can be transformed, step by step, into the kingdom of God" (38). The anti-Christ figure in *The Lord of the World* becomes the "Man-God," the "Lord of the World," precisely by promising universal brotherhood, peace, and love, but no transcendence.

The hero of the book is an English priest, Percy Franklin, who looks almost exactly like the mysterious Julian Felsenburgh, who is an American senator from, yes, Vermont. He suddenly appears as a lone and dramatic figure promising the world goodness if it but follow him. No one quite knows who he is or where he is from, but his voice mesmerizes. Under his leadership, East and West join. War is abolished. Felsenburgh becomes the President of Europe, then of the World, by popular acclaim. Everyone is fascinated with him. Still no one knows much about him. People are both riveted and frightened by the way he demands attention. Most follow without question.

The only groups who in any sense oppose him are the few loyal Catholics. The English priest is eventually called to Rome since he has been an acute observer of the rise of Felsenburgh and his agenda. Apostasies among bishops and priests increase. The Pope is a good man, John XXIV, not unlike Pius X, who was pope when this novel was written. Belief in God is to be replaced by belief in man. All those who oppose this doctrine are slated for extermination. With the English priest's inspiration, the Pope forms a new religious order, the Order of Christ Crucified. Its members, including the Pope, vow to die in the name of the faith. Many do.

The English Prime Minister and his wife form a sub-plot. The wife desperately wants to believe in this new world movement. But she is horrified when she sees the killings that are justified in the name of world unity. The Prime Minister's mother, meantime, was brought back to the faith by the English priest, much to the horror of the Prime Minister. But the wife is upset at the whole thing. Finally, to escape it all, she applies for and is granted public euthanasia. She dies not believing but somehow knowing that what is coming with Felsenburgh is utterly horrible.

As the world comes to an end, the Pope calls all the cardinals to Rome. Meantime, some English Catholics, against orders, plot to blow up the Abbey where the politicians meet. Percy Franklin, now a cardinal, with a German cardinal, are sent back home to try to prevent this plot which they are warned about. But word gets out. In retaliation, Felsenburgh orders that Rome be destroyed, which it is, together with the pope and all the cardinals but the three are not in Rome. These three quickly elect the younger Englishman as the new pope, Sylvester III. The old cardinal in Jerusalem dies. The German cardinal is hanged.

The last pope goes to the Holy Land, to the places of the last days pictured in the New Testament. In a final act, Felsenburgh and all the world leaders fly in formation to destroy the remaining signs of faith on earth. In response, Sylvester and the remaining Catholics are at Mass. As they sing together the music of Benediction, the *Tantum Ergo*, the attack strikes. With that, at the same time the world ends.

The last words of the novel are: "Then this world passed, and the glory of it." It could not be more dramatic, or more moving. Somehow, I no longer find it so frightening. It is almost consoling.

Chapter 5
ON THE IMPARTIAL READING OF BOOKS

In #82 of *The Rambler* for Tuesday 15 January 1751, Samuel John-son wrote: "So prevalent is the habit of comparing ourselves with others, while they remain within the reach of our passions, that books are seldom read with complete impartiality, but by those from whom the writer is placed at such a distance that his life or death is indifferent." Who did Johnson intend by "those within the reach of our passions?" He implied that envy, hatred, adulation, greed, or pride can cloud our judgment when we compare ourselves to those with whom we interact.

The vice of envy, in particular, is more frequent among us than we generally realize. It is more damaging than greed, a distant com-petitor. Envy is quite present in academia, where the competition is of a spiritual or intellectual nature. But, in this regard, the culture of modern media might give it a run for its money.

Some economists indeed have considered envy to be a major factor in economic relations, more so than greed or self-interest. Issues revolving around poverty in particular are often more ex-plained by envy than greed. Efforts to deal with the poor almost always fail because they assume that the issue of why the poor are poor is one of greed and not one of envy.

Greed is the vice of wanting material goods out of proportion to our real needs and abilities. Since money enables us to buy al-most anything, we can make it our end. We think that this accu-mulation (or lack) of wealth is what happiness is all about. We associate greed mostly with the rich but it can also be a vice preva-lent among the poor, even the very poor.

Envy, on the other hand, is more spiritual. It consists in honors and glory. We do not praise what should be praised in others. We find fault with the excellence or performance of other people because, well, we hate their guts. We choose not freely to give credit where or in what excellence it is manifest. We do not like what we see when we "compare ourselves with others." The vice of Judas might well have been greed, but that of the Pharisees was more certainly that of envy. To give honor and praise where they are due is much more difficult and much more important than in giving or returning money where it is due.

The fact is that I read neither Plato nor Aristotle "impartially," even though they died considerably before my time. To be educated, even today, especially today, one has to take a stand with regard to Plato and Aristotle. Yet, if that affirmation were accepted, all universities would insist that Plato and Aristotle be read by those matriculating in them. They don't.

Those who know Plato and Aristotle are often envied with a passion verging on hatred. These ancient gentlemen stand for the truth. They make it clear. Our historic civilization is built, as I like to say, on the Socratic proposition that "It is never right to do wrong." No statement is more hated in a modern relativist world. None is more envied by those who refuse to admit its truth. They have no other choice.

Yet, what does it mean to "read a book with 'complete impartiality'"? It means that we can read the book without our protective mind interfering to prevent us from admitting the truth of what opposes what we want to do. Our current society is full of a hatred rooted in envy, in the refusal to acknowledge the truth of our being. We are thus in a revolutionary situation, something similar to what Burke described in his *Reflections on the Revolution in France*. We have now freely chosen principles of polity that deny elements of goodness in our being. We do not bind ourselves to *what is*. We withhold praise from any truth that we choose not to live by.

The "anti-hate" laws that now prevail in Canada, Britain, and this country are themselves rooted in an envy and hatred of any truth that contradicts currently established ideology. Freedom of speech, whose root justification was the obligation to speak and listen to the truth, has become an instrument to exclude any consideration of truths that conflict with what we want as we politically will it.

We are now far enough away from Scripture and the classical authors whereby we might objectively consider them. But it has not turned out this way. Why we wonder? I think it is because the articulation of the truth requires these two sources to see it. If our "passions" do not allow us to admit their truth, we end up hating it because we cannot but envy its existence. The refusal to praise what is true and good is increasingly the ethos of our culture.

Chapter 6
ON PLEASURES OF OUR KIND

A friend sent an old *Peanuts* cartoon strip with a 1964 United Features copyright. Sally is diligently writing her history homework paper. Charlie Brown looks on. She writes: "Britain was invaded in the year 43 by Roman Numerals." To be funny, Charlie says to her: "They probably had them outnumbered." In the next frame, Sally, with a reputation for not getting it, abruptly turns to Charlie, "What?" Somewhat deflated, Charlie mutters "Nothing." To which Sally replies, in a classic response which proves that she is sharper than Charlie suspected: "It's a pleasure never to know what you're talking about!"

This sequence reminds me of a story my younger brother once told me when our father was still alive. I had given copies of some articles I had published at the time to my astonished family. Evidently my father took a look at them, as did my brother. I was off in Europe at the time. One day my father, talking about these literary feats, asked my brother: "Do you know what the hell he is talking about?" To which my brother, I am sure, replied in words not un-similar to Sally's.

The whole point of conversation and its pleasure is to understand what someone else is talking about. It is true that occasionally we would just as soon not know what someone is talking about. I remember reading once a comment of the famous Sidney Hook, who said that we would just as soon not know certain things about someone else, like he betrayed his friend or country.

The topic of pleasure is a rather good one. It never much occurs to us that it is also something to think about. We know its worth from experience, if we cannot figure out how to formulate it. There is pleasure and thought about pleasure, both. Aristotle writes well on this topic. To know what pleasure is, probably is the first step in enabling us to put it in the right order of our souls. Even when we know the purpose of pleasure, it does not follow that we will do the right thing by it. As Aristotle implies, it can be separated from its natural purpose. It can be "used" as if it had no purpose or could be bent to our purpose any way we wanted it to.

We find as many different pleasures as we have things to do normally—eating, sleeping, drinking, smelling, love-making, knowing, or remembering. Each of these activities has its own proper pleasure. Pleasure ought not to be something we seek for its own sake apart from its purpose. If we do this separation, we will always get it wrong. The goodness or badness of pleasure is not the pleasure itself, but the nature of the act in which it exists. If the act is good, the pleasure is good. Pleasures are already there, given with the being we are. We do not make them to be what they are. We either use them well or badly. How we deal with our pleasures—and our sufferings—pretty much indicates what sort of person we are.

Historically, a few influential Stoics have tried to make pleasure as such bad. It was never a popular opinion. It was a dangerous one, none the less. No one doubts that, if not controlled, pleasure can deflect us from our proper good. Aristotle had a pungent remark about politicians. If they did know and seek a higher kind of pleasure connected with truth and beauty, they would likely embrace disordered pleasures. Nothing in our present political experience indicates that Aristotle was wrong.

Yet, some men are too good for ordinary pleasures. Scripture tells us that when we fast or give alms, we need to be pretty careful. Our good deeds can be occasions for pride and vanity. I have liked to meditate on the devil, not a full time occupation, to be sure. He is one creature that is not influenced by carnal or physical pleasure. The most dangerous of our kind imitate him. We should not be surprised at this. This is why the kind of pleasure that comes with pride is not proper to our kind. It is the distortion of the pleasure due to knowing the truth.

The liberally educated person is classically defined as someone who knows and experiences the right pleasure in each activity, right time, place, and proportion. Ignatius of Loyola suggested that if we were excessive in something, we should bend towards the opposite extreme to reach a balance. Aristotle said the same thing. We need to moderate our pleasures to enjoy them.

"A pleasure never to know what you are talking about?" This pleasure, I suspect, arises only when we do, finally, know what we are talking about.

Chapter 7

On Nothingness

The classic statement reads: *Ex nihilo, nihil fit*—from nothing, nothing happens. This affirmation cannot be "proved." It is a "first" thing, a first "principle." Nothing is clearer that could make it even clearer. A "proof" would require something more evident than this principle itself. We cannot deny it without, at the same time, implicitly affirming it. If I say "something comes from nothing," or "nothing from something," I indicate that I have not understood what "nothing" means.

We do not encounter "nothing" walking down the streets. We only encounter "somethings," this thing or that thing. The very notion of "nothing" requires that we already know that something *exists*. To understand the meaning of "nothing," we must mentally deny an existing thing its "is-ness." The resulting concept enables us to have some notion of "nothing." We never actually encounter a "nothing"—a "nobody" perhaps, but that implies something else.

So we ask: "Why is there something and not just nothing?" We cannot *not* ask this question and remain rationally whole. If "nothing" is what it says it is, namely, *no*-thing, we figure that something must come from something. This "something" that it comes from must itself come from something or else it must be something that simply "is" by itself. A self-contained "is-ness" would be the source of *all that is*. It would be at the heart of anything that appears out of nothingness.

It is possible that "nothing" might "exist" except for a "self-contained, uncaused is-ness." The world as we know it need not exist. Neither the world itself nor we in it seeking to understand it need to exist. If we do exist, as we do, we already are what we are through some origin not our own. Our thinking about our existence does not in fact lead us to "nothingness."

We live in a culture that, without contradicting itself, would like to deny what is implied here. Many would prefer, as they think, a world that came from "nothing." That origin, it is assumed, would simplify things. We would only have to be responsible to ourselves. We would be "free" of any "claims" on us to be something we do not "want" to be. This alternative means that we need to affirm that nothing can be found in *what is* that requires a "cause," an "outside" explanation.

Behind such reflection is the nagging suspicion that we still want our origin in "nothingness" to be "true." But if it is "true," why are we around thinking that we must "prove," at least to ourselves, that we do not originate from *what is existence* itself? We want it both ways. We do exist. That is clear to us. If we face "nothing," it is definitely we "not nothings" who face it.

In the last book of the *Republic*, Plato spoke of the immortality of the soul. The reason he did this was to answer the question of whether the world was created in injustice. Since many sins and crimes went unpunished in this life and many good deeds unrewarded, it was clear that, without a final judgment, the world was created in injustice.

If this abiding injustice were so, it did not make any difference what we did. Both the just and the unjust, if there could be such, would eventually end in nothingness. Nothing we did really makes any difference or even makes sense. But if we really existed and if our actions made an ultimate difference, then nothingness is not our end.

"Nothingness" is but a desperate attempt to escape our acknowledging *what we are*. Why should we want to deny the kind of existence that we have been given? Human existence includes a freedom that can reject *what man is*. But the trajectory of this rejection does not lead to "nothingness." It leads to abiding existence in a permanent state of self-enclosure.

What is said of Judas can be said of all who follow his path: "It would be better had he not been born" (Mark 14:8). Once born, "nothingness" is no longer an alternative except in an imagination that prefers it to *what is*. But the one who chooses this "nothingness" is not ultimately returned to "nothing." Once we are conceived and born, our destiny is never "nothingness." It is either eternal life or eternal doom.

Chesterton quoted his grandfather to say: "He would thank God for his existence even if he ended in hell." Hell is not "nothingness." It is rather "somethingness" that preferred "nothingness" to that glory which, like existence itself, was freely offered to it. God, in the beginning, was free not to create. But once free beings were in existence, though He tried, He was not able to prevent all of them from choosing "nothingness." He could not make them, at the same time, free and not free, immortal and "nothing."

Chapter 8
ON THE BELLOC SUSSEX WALK OF 1902

Each year from October 29 to All Souls' Day, I like to reread Belloc's wonderful book, *The Four Men*. I used to have the Oxford University paperback edition, but, all marked up, it fell apart, much to my dismay. Happily, one of my former students, James Crowley of Chicago, managed to find a handsome hard-back edition from Thomas Nelson and Sons in London. It is unfortunately undated, but it contains many of Belloc's original drawings along with the musical notes and songs that are interspersed in the book.

At the Washington Belloc Society Meetings, Scott Block often leads the merry group through a hearty rendition of these songs. As I cannot read music, I often wondered how the musical notes in the book sounded. I once had a student from Waterbury, Connecticut, I think, who now teaches Gaelic Literature at the University of Cork in Ireland. He played the book's music for me at the piano in the Jesuit Residence at Georgetown. He also sang it. I asked him how he knew how to play and sing. "My grandmother was a jazz pianist," he told me.

The original Nelson edition of *The Four Men* was published in 1923. My copy, also falling apart with age, looks old enough to be an original. Reproductions of this Nelson edition are still available. The book contains 310 pages, divided into five chapter days—the Twenty-ninth of October 1902, the Thirtieth of October, the Thirty-First of October, the First of November, and the Second of November. These are All Hallow' Eve, All Hallows' Day, and the Day of the Dead. The book is a meditation on home, on life and death, on companionship and its loss. The book, like Belloc himself, is at the same time sad and rollicking, nostalgic and prophetic, funny and solemn.

No book is quite like this book, except perhaps Belloc's more famous 1901 walk (*The Path to Rome*) that began at his old army quarters in Toul in France—Belloc was half-French and served in the French Army. Recording at each step what he saw of Europe and its Faith, he proceeded over the Alps and down through Italy to arrive in time for High Mass at St. Peter's on the Feast of Saints Peter and Paul (June 29). He vowed never to change his boots, or to take any vehicular assistance, vows, and the letter of which he kept. Thereby, he gave us a lesson in casuistry and moral theology—*odiosa sunt restringenda*, that is, if the law is not in one's favor, it is to be interpreted strictly.

Thus, it is up to the lawgiver to state exactly what he meant, not to the observer of the law to guess. Belloc made it to Rome all right and even to St. Peter's Square (which is really circular). But he decided to have lunch instead. In the name of every reader, he asked if he was not going to say anything about Rome itself. "No," he said. This book is called *The Path to Rome*, not to be missed in this life, if you want to live this life as it ought to be lived.

The "four men" are all Belloc—Belloc as a Sailor, as a Poet, as an old man (one Grizzlebeard), and as himself, i.e., Myself. Belloc sailed a boat, wrote poetry, grew old and was always Belloc. Sussex, where the walk took place, is his active county in southern England where his home was in King's Land. He died on July 16, 1953. His mother was English; his wife was an American from Napa, California. He lost a son in both World War I and World War II. He seems to know every town, hill, woods, bridge, and river of the County, as well as its history and its lore. Sussex, he tells us, was in local legend the original Garden of Eden. Along the way, we meet St. Dunstan who led the Devil on with tongs, and St. Lenard. We learn of the Inns of the world. There is nothing so great as an Inn, we are told, convincingly, I must say.

The book begins with Belloc in the "George," an Inn at Robertsbridge. He is drinking port. I must add that the drinking of beer and ale, of port and brandy, the dining on eggs and bacon, on cottage loaves and the cheese of Stilton form the background of this walk. One is almost always hungry just reading of its frequent culinary passages. And the book is full of songs—of old Catholic songs, to wit: "May all good fellows that here agree / Drink Audit Ale in heaven with me, / And may all my enemies go to hell! / Noel! Noel! Noel! Noel!"

The theme of home—"What is it?" "Where is it?"—pervades the book. "Whatever you read in the all the writings of men, and whatever you hear in all the speech of men, and whatever you notice in the eyes of men, of express or reminiscence or desire, you will see nothing in any man's speech or writing or expression to match that which marks his hunger for home." In the very last lines of the book, after the walk and the breaking of companionship, he returns to the Downs and home, not without recalling Homer and Odysseus, the smoke from the chimney seen from a distance.

There are passages in this book that I dearly love. In a way, the thesis of the book is that we cannot really keep anything in this world unless perhaps we remember it, even write about it. All things will change. What our county was like when we were but lads will not be quite the same when we are old. The book begins: "My County, it has been proved in the life of every man that though his loves are human, and therefore changeable, yet in proportion as he attaches them to things unchangeable, so they mature and broaden." Belloc teaches us to look for the permanent things midst our passing days. But are there any examples of this change midst loveable things? Are there any images by which we can see what is at stake?

"On this account, Dear Sussex, are those women chiefly dear to men who, as the seasons pass, do but continue to be more and more themselves, attain balance, and abandon or forget vicissitude." The walk, as I said, is full of the passingness of things. Indeed, at one point, the four men ask themselves "What is the 'worst' thing in the world?" The poet says that it is an "earache." But the old man, Grizzlebeard, says this is nonsense. The worst thing in the world is "the passing of human affection." This passing is worse than the death of friends which is not voluntary. The bond of human affection is nothing if it is not voluntary. When it is broken, we are somehow broken with it, as the history of all true love and friendship testifies to us.

But after they consider what the worst thing is, they take up the related question: "What is best?" "For in the midst of this world, where everything is happy except man, and where the night should teach us quiet, we ought to learn or discover what the best thing in the world is." Why, we wonder, is everything happy except man? It is because man cannot be happy unless he chooses the good; he is never coerced. He often choses wrongly. "I am a little puzzled in this point," Myself, that is, Belloc, continues: "Why, if most men follow their satisfaction, most men come to so wretched an end?" It is because of sloth, *aecedia*, that capital vice that makes us interested in everything but what is really important, in the salvation of our souls and the life that is described as eternal.

But I shall tell no more of this amazing book here lest any reader should judge that by reading these words of Schall he has really read the book. 'Tis not and cannot be so. Why? At one point, the Poet tells Myself that, in all the stories, "even in the story of the homecoming of Ulysses, they do not dare to tell you all the human things that followed and all the incompletion of its joys." Myself responds that if he can finally come back to the rivers of his home county—the Lavant, the Rother, and the Arun—that he "will live there gracefully as if I were the fruit of it, and die there as easily as a fruit falls, and be buried in it and mix with it for ever, and leave myself and all I had to it for an inheritance."

When the four men finally end their journey at the border of the County Sussex, on the morning of All Souls' Day, they agree to break a loaf in silence and each go his own way. They stood in silence "for about the time in which a man can say good-bye with reverence." The last piece of advice that the four men hear is from Grizzlebeard. On their walk they have spoken of the important things already. "But I who am old will give you advice, which is this—to consider chiefly from now onward those permanent things which are, as it were, the shores of this age and the harbours of our glittering and pleasant but dangerous and wholly changeful sea." With such words they leave one another, their brief companionship. In the "gathering darkness," Myself, Belloc, turns "southward across the Downs to my home." This is, as I said, a book not to be missed in this world.

Chapter 9

ON AQUINAS AND MODERNITY

After Vatican II, the modern Catholic wanted finally to be reconciled with the good things that were said to have come about because of modernity or the modern mind, or modern technology. Aquinas (d. 1274), to be sure, is famous for his ability to see the good that is contained in the remaining "being" of anything that lacks its complete good. Aquinas, the most respected of Catholic thinkers, is thus pictured as saving the good things of modern times from the backwardness of those not open enough or liberal enough to accept modern science or thought. Faith is true only insofar as it accepts science. It has no independent ground to question science's or reason's affirmations.

If this essay were entitled, "The Modernity of Aquinas," moreover, it would imply that Aquinas already knew what this world had itself later discovered. In this case, Aquinas would be seen as a prophet. It could, however, also imply that something was lost or never yet discovered in Aquinas that could now provide a remedy to this modernity that increasingly shows incompleteness, if not downright derangement. In this latter case, we would find in Aquinas something found no place else, something vital for our well being.

In reading the *Commentary* on Aristotle's *Metaphysics* of Aquinas, I was struck by the number of times in this text that sentences began with the words: The truth is that..., or, The truth of the matter is.... These words are mindful of John Paul II's *Fides et Ratio*. They indicate that the purpose of our mind is not "doubt" but precisely truth. The mind is capable, after its own manner, of knowing all things. What is not ourselves becomes ours through our power of knowing. We do not directly know ourselves. We begin to know by confronting what is not ourselves, beginning with any particular, sensible, ordinary thing.

We live in an age that, except, ironically, for that affirmation itself, claims not to know the truth. It does not think truth is possible. The modern mind has lost its confidence precisely as mind. The result is that we speak, and are allowed to speak, of truth only in the context of "toleration." That is, we must cover all our affirmations with the gloss of doubt. All thought is equal. All ideas have the same validity. Therefore, we cannot impose our truth. Truth is not one, but multiple. That is, it does not exist. Contradictory truths are not only possible, but politically mandatory. As Hume said, the opposite of every matter of fact is possible. That is in this hypothesis, if I say you sit before me, and you do sit before me, it is possible that you do *not* so sit before me. Minds do not reach realities. The opposite of what they see is always possible

What is the essence of modernity? It is that there is no objective order, either in our souls or in the universe. The mind is conscious. But it knows nothing but itself. Therefore, the external world, including the inwardness of others of our kind, is not something we discover but only something we project and enforce. We do now know the same truths. We do not live in common in the same reality whereby we can mutually check the validity of our knowing.

Rather we prefer to live in whatever world we will into existence. Choice creates reality; it does not select it. We are autonomous. We are free to be anything except what we are. We thus do not allow fanaticism. That is, we marginalize, ostracize, or ignore any claim to know the truth, to say that: The truth is this or that. In a world of doubt, the only fanaticism is, to recall Plato, the truth itself. That is: *To say of what is that it is, to say of what is not, that it is not.*

Thomas Aquinas read Aristotle (d. 322 B.C.) carefully. He read Scripture, Augustine, and the philosophers, again carefully. He began with things, with *what is*. He reflectively examined our knowing powers. He wanted to know the order of things, including human things, divine things. He did not think that if something was true in his time, it could not be true in some other time, say, in our time. He was not a cultural relativist or a historicist, that is, someone who confined truth to culture or time. On the contrary, if something is indeed true in one time, it is true in every time and indeed in every place.

Aquinas, furthermore, did not think that revelation was private, nor did he think it was subjective. Rather he thought that it was directed to our very minds. The basic truths of revelation, that is, Creation, Incarnation, and Redemption, could be intellectually recognized, however, only if we already, from reason and experience, had formulated in our minds the questions to which what is revealed was the answer. Aquinas, in other words, did not think that the content of revelation was purely subjective faith. He thought that if it was in fact an answer to questions that men wondered about in every age and nation, ones they constantly asked themselves about, such revelational answers could not be excluded from consideration.

Indeed, Aquinas thought that revelation made it possible to think better. We hear it said that if something comes from faith, it is of no use or interest to those who do not or cannot believe. Aquinas did not think this way. He thought that if revelation answered some query or enigma that reason formulated but could not answer, it must mean that there was a strange coherence or unity in the universe. Things built on things. One truth led to another. Grace built on nature.

Autonomous modernity does not listen to Aquinas because it has, as it thinks, refuted him. It does not listen to him because it chooses not to listen to its own mind, to its own questions that arise from *what is*. Aquinas is not a modern man because he does not know modern truth built only on our will. He is not a modern man because modern men choose not to know the truth itself, the truth about themselves, or the truth revealed to them.

Chapter 10

On Travel

Francis Bacon (1561–1600) wrote a famous essay, "On Travel." It begins with the words: "Travel, in the younger sort, is a part of education; in the elder, a part of experience. He that travelleth into a country before he has some entrance into the language goeth to school, not to travel." Experience is what happens to us when we encounter something that actually exists, something we could not know about in any other way but, as it were, by being there. This "experience" is supported by, kept by, our memory so that we know that this thing did happen.

Travel, no doubt, is a world-wide industry, though somewhat crippled and certainly made less comfortable by today's security in air travel. Bacon, no doubt, lived in days before simultaneous translations and widespread knowledge of other languages in the land into which we travel. "English spoken here" is no doubt a sign in any major hotel or store almost anywhere in the world. But it is true that we can have little "experience" without the "language." We can, to be sure, see Mt. Fuji in all its beauty without knowing Japanese. But we can hardly know what it means to the Japanese without knowing Japanese.

Bacon assumed that when we go to another country, we would actually meet someone there with whom we would wish to continue acquaintance. "When a traveller returneth home, let him not leave the countries where he hath travelled altogether behind him, but maintain a correspondence by letters with those of his acquaintance which are of more worth...." Bacon thought that purchasing a beret in France, lederhosen in Germany, or an outback hat in Australia would not do it. Real acquaintance meant real letters. And suddenly employing some foreign phrases or gestures will seem odd to his own friends on his return. Bacon is not against incorporating some foreign things into one's local habits or language, but he thinks they should only be choice "flowers."

When I again came across this essay of Bacon "On Travel," I had a nagging memory of another phrase, to wit, "Travel narrows the mind." Aristotle had said that some acquaintance with foreign manners and habits would prevent us from being too much concentrated on ourselves. Travel, he thought, will enable us to be more judicious and understanding of what goes on in human nature.

I was pretty sure that the expression "travel narrows a mind" was from Chesterton, but I was not sure. So I looked it up on a search engine. Sure enough, it is found in the first paragraph of an essay, "What Is America?," in his *What I Saw in America*. Chesterton did not think that travel was all that educative. Indeed, he thought the average Englishman in his suburb of Hampstead or Surbiton had more sympathy for the Laplanders, Chinamen, and Patagonians of this world if he stayed at home than if he travelled and actually met one or other of these distinguished gentlemen or gentle ladies.

When we are at home, Chesterton thought, we feel a certain bond for other human beings in distant lands.

> Man is inside all men. In a real sense any man may be inside any man. But to travel is to leave the inside and draw dangerously near the outside. So long as he thought of men in the abstract, like naked toiling figures in some classic frieze, merely as those who labor and love their children and die, he was thinking the fundamental truth about them. By going to look at their unfamiliar manners and customs he is inviting them to disguise themselves in fantastic masks and costumes. Many modern internationalists talk as if men of different nationalities had only to meet and mix and understand each other. In reality, that is the moment of supreme danger–the moment when they meet.

Notice that Chesterton, for his part, says exactly the opposite of what we would expect. We long, so we think, to know real men in their concrete circumstances but when we first encounter the odd ways in which they do things, when we do not know their language, we initially suspect that they are barely human. Abstractions, on the other hand, are often more real than reality. Indeed, as Aristotle had said long ago in his ongoing conversation with Plato, we derive the abstractions from the widely differing, but somehow recognizable, uniformities or forms in the realities we encounter in our travels.

Chesterton thinks that seeing the world narrowed us, though even he writes these words while traveling in America. "Travel ought to combine amusement with instruction," Chesterton continues; "But most travelers are so much amused that they refuse to be instructed. I do not blame them for being amused; it is perfectly natural to be amused at a Dutchman for being Dutch or a Chinaman for being Chinese." Notice, however, that Chesterton sees nothing impossible in gaining "experience," to use Bacon's term, or "instruction," to use his own term, while at the same time being amused at what we see.

Bacon thinks that on going on a journey, we should go with a tutor who knows his way around so that we do not have to waste time on finding out what is important to see. The only trouble with this view, however, as far as I can see, is that very often the best insights we get into people and places are when we are outside of what is considered most important to see. With a tutor, we will never, I suspect, be too surprised. It is perfectly natural being amused by a Dutchman being Dutch.

Bacon also thinks that it was odd that when people traveled by sea, they kept diaries where there was nothing to observe but water, but when they traveled by land, which was full of things to observe, "for the most part they omit" writing down what they encounter.

Chesterton is able to see the essentials of life from one's own home in Hampstead or Surbiton—not that Chesterton did not himself travel. He warns, in another place, of the Englishman who, when he travels to Rome, sees only what he saw at home. That is, he is mindful of the Japanese traveler who will only eat in Japanese restaurants when he is in San Francisco or Hamburg, or the American who dines exclusively at McDonald's in Paris. But Chesterton knows that in spite of the wildness of gesture and dress and habit, underneath everything are birth and love, work and death, no matter what they might look like on the outside. If we see the outside and miss the inside, we will likely think that all foreigners are a bunch of Hottentots or even men from Mars.

Finally, to return to Bacon, what should we look at when we travel? "The things to be seen and observed are," Bacon observed—and I will add numbers to them, just to stress their variety:

> 1) Courts of princes, especially when they give audiences to ambassadors; 2) the courts of justice, while they sit and hear causes; 3) and so of consistories ecclesiastic; 4) the churches and the monasteries, with monuments which are therein extant; 5) the walls and fortifications of cities and towns; 6) and so the havens and harbours, 7) antiquities and ruins, 8) libraries, 9) colleges, 10) disputations, 11) and lectures, where any are; 12) shipping and navies; 13) houses and gardens of state and pleasure, near great cities; 14) armories, 15) arsenals, 16) magazines, 17) exchanges, 18) burses, 19) warehouses, 20) exercises of horsemanship, 21) fencing, 22) training of soldiers, and the like; 23) comedies, such whereunto the better sort of persons do resort, 24) treasuries of jewels and robes' 25) cabinets and rarities; 26) and, to conclude, whatsoever is memorable in the places where they go.

Needless to say, this is quite a list. But it is not quite all, "as for triumphs, masks, feasts, weddings, funerals, capital executions, and such shows, men need not to be put in mind of them: yet are they not to be neglected?"

Thus, travel can "narrow the mind" if we only see the outside of things. We need not be "put in mind," as Bacon put it, of certain "shows"–like funerals and capital executions, though they too are not to be "neglected." We may in our travel be amused by the comedies "Whereunto the better sort of persons does resort." Many modern internationalists naively talk as if men of different nationalities had only "to meet and mix" to understand each other. We travel when young to know the language, to be educated. We travel as elders for experience. Man is "inside all men." The fundamental truth of all men is that they "labor and love their children and die."

Chapter 11
ON "CATHOLIC" UNIVERSITIES

A young Brazilian, whom I do not know, sent me an e-mail. He told me that he dropped out of the Catholic University there at which he was matriculating when the theology professor denied the real presence, scorned liturgical norms, and nixed the reality of the resurrection of Christ. "Who pays this teacher's salary!" we wonder. But one may not need to go to Brazil to find such professors or positions.

I often am annoyed at the uncritical use of modern concepts of "human rights" and "values" as if they are perfectly compatible with either a realistic philosophy or revelation. Such notions originate in modern philosophy. Generally, they mean whatever we want them to mean, except what Christians think that they mean.

When I complained of this confusion to a friend, he replied: "The heart and soul of ecclesiastical rhetoric is based on the conflation of Christianity with secular humanitarianism, with what Comte so suggestively called 'the religion of humanity.'" This "religion of humanity," however it is called, is the practical alternative to orthodoxy in the modern world. I would say "alternative to Christianity" but so many Christians in practice actually worship the "religion of humanity" that I hesitate to use it.

Such thoughts came to mind as, with a class, I read the 1993 essay of Father Ernest Fortin, A. A. entitled: "Do We Need Catholic Universities?" Fortin was a man of remarkable insight, much too seldom studied. He begins with a critique of Msgr. John Tracy Ellis' famous essay of 1955, "American Catholics and the Intellectual Life."

Fortin found the presuppositions of this essay dubious. The criterion of what a university should be was taken from the standards of the secular university. The publication of this essay, in many minds, was the justification to go about hiring and using standard evaluations that no longer had a Catholic component. "Excellence" was something that consisted in imitating what the "prestigious universities" do.

Fortin discovered that students from a few Catholic schools, usually small ones, were in fact receiving a much more liberal education than was found in the secular universities or larger Catholic universities. But these smaller schools mostly had to go it alone. The situation today is even more striking. The norm of the university is no longer just a "secular" university but a "research" university. This is, as it were, where the money is.

"Why is it that the bulk of the education provided at such great cost to both graduates and undergraduates by our best schools," Fortin wondered, "is so often perceived by the students themselves as anemic and antiseptic to the nth degree?" Fortin's comment echoes one of Allan Bloom's, namely, that the unhappiest students today are found in twenty or thirty "best" and most expensive universities. In their teeming minds, they find that they have arrived at the "best" schools, spent all this money, but are left basically empty of soul.

Fortin goes on with his explanation: "The reason, I suppose, is that most faculty members are themselves products of the modern research university and imbued with its peculiar ethos." "What is this peculiar ethos?" we inquire. It is this: We do our research on man without knowing what man is. Indeed, we presuppose or claim we have proved that no human nature exists. Hence no limits on science or on our "research" can be found.

Leo Strauss had it right: "The conquest of nature requires the conquest of human nature and hence in the first place the questioning of the unchangeability of human nature: an unchangeable human nature might set absolute limits to progress" (*The City and Man*). It is this "progress" to which our universities are addicted in their "research."

We set about "creating" a new man and a new humanity. We have given up on virtue with the discipline and grace needed both to understand and practice it. We do not just "lower our sights." In our complete autonomy from nature and reason, we accept nothing but what we first will.

"By and large," Fortin remarked, "philosophy and theology have been stripped of their status as architectonic disciplines and survive, if they survive at all, as parts of a democratic arrangement within which the quest for first principles and the unity of knowledge are dismissed not only as irrelevant but as inimical to the modern egalitarian ideals." We now study and promote "diversity" for its own sake. We cannot seek the transcendent good, true, and beautiful lest they restrict our "progress" by implying that "not all is permitted," to recall Dostoyevsky and Socrates.

We have universities that study everything but what we are and might be in reason and grace. We "research" all that is but *what is.* The highest things cannot be thus "researched." This is why we are said to be free. Yet, the old dictum holds. Only the truth makes us free. If we cannot admit this, we really cannot be free.

Chapter 12

ON THE TEMPTATION TO ORGANIZE THE WORLD

Ogden Nash has a poem that begins: "A man could be granted to live a dozen lives / And he still wouldn't be understood by daughters and wives...." We probably wouldn't want a world in which it were otherwise, a world in which absolutely everything could be understood by husbands and wives. I do not intend to defend mystery here or the finiteness of our intellects, designed to know all that is. Rather I want to reflect on what it would mean to claim that we know everything, especially that we create the distinction between good and evil.

On John Paul II's visit to Poland (June 6, 1999), he took a helicopter to a sea port called Elblag, a city of about 130,000 people. Improbably, in Elblag, they had an "Aviation Club," where the Pope participated in devotions at which he recited "the Act of Consecration of the Human Race to the Sacred Heart of Jesus." Makes you wonder that if the Holy Father can consecrate the human race at the Aviation Club in Elblag, it could be done in any parish in the States or world.

John Paul II explained that "Everything that God wanted to tell us about himself and about his love he placed in the Heart of Jesus, and by means of that Heart he has told us everything." This sentence does not refer to our own views of the world, our own opinions of the important things. What is important is what "God wanted to tell us about himself." The first thing that those who love God must do, recalling John 14:15, is to keep the commandments. The Ten Commandments are the "foundation of morality." And just to remind us, he proceeds to recite all Ten Commandments, a good practice.

Christ confirmed these commandments at the Sermon on the Mount. The "whole order of truth" is "inscribed on the human heart." The Pope cited the passages that Christ used to reaffirm the commandments: "I have come not to abolish them (the law and the prophets) but to fulfill them" (Matthew 5:17); "He who has my commandments and keeps them, he it is who loves me; and he who loves me will be loved by my Father" (John 14:21). John Paul finally cites the passage he loves from Matthew 19:16, the passage that he reflected on in *Veritatis Splendor*, where the young man asks, "Teacher, what good deed must I do to have eternal life?" Jesus answers, "If you would enter life, keep the commandments."

At this point, John Paul II paused in his homily to remind us that "This response by Jesus is particularly important for modern reality, in which many people live as though there were no God." This "living as if there were no God" is not something neutral, or abstract, but something contemporary, quite widespread, perhaps world-wide. It is not just a question of men not being understood by their wives and daughters, but of God being positively rejected.

In what sounds to be a modern "Aviation Club" during what seem like early modern devotions, the Pole adds these profound words: "The temptation to organize the world and one's own life without God or even in opposition to God, without his commandments and without the Gospel, is a very real temptation and threatens us too. When human life and the world are built without God, they will eventually turn against man himself" (*L'Osservatore Romano*, English, 16 June 1999).

So a temptation to "organize" ourselves and the world on principles that ignore or reject the Commandments does exist among us. We are in fact pursuing this goal more and more in our civil laws and personal practices. Once we posit our own will as the source of law and action, as we are free to do, we proceed to live as we choose. No Pope who knows his theology, as John Paul II certainly does, can be surprised that this possibility exists. But notice what he says about this possibility. Whom can it hurt? God? It does indeed hurt God through hurting those He loves.

The crux of the issue is that when we build our lives and that of our society without God, without the Commandments, such lives will "turn against man." That is, they will turn against those who observe the commandments. It is probably no accident that this turning seems almost complete in our public order and that, correspondingly, the Pope frequently talks about martyrdom. Even if we are granted a dozen lives, even if Lazarus returns from the grave, it will not be otherwise if we do not observe the Commandments, because we deny by our choices and actions the validity of the law of God in our hearts.

Chapter 13
ON ANSWERS

One does not have to be around universities very long before one encounters the notion that "questioning" is the real "reason" for education. "We 'question' everything" actually becomes a reason given for going to such an institution as a university. Actually, it is a better reason to stay away from it. Poor Socrates is pictured as wandering around the streets of Athens blithely asking questions with great abandon. Aquinas is famous for asking some ten thousand questions in the *Summa* alone. Lord knows how many more appear in his other works. From all sides, including churchmen, we hear of dialogue, of questioning our basic "values."

But if we ask the question—"Why do we ask questions?"—the proper response is not so that we can ask more questions. It is rather so that we can find an answer to our question. It may be quite true that the answer to one question leads to another question, even when the answer is a real answer. That is, only if it is true. Obviously, if the answer is not true, new questions will, even more pressingly, arise.

The purpose of mind is not to broadcast a kind of universal fuzziness in which everyone goes about affirming "I don't know" to every conceivable issue. The simple fact is that there are things that we do and should know. If we, like the famous political party, "know nothing," we are barely human. Even Descartes, when he set out to doubt everything, did so in order to find something that he could not doubt—which turned out to be himself thinking. On this basis, he hoped to build a world bereft of doubt.

In the Gospels, Mary asks questions—"How can this be?" So does Christ—"Who do men say that I am?." Both get or give answers. Philosophers tell us that in the beginning our minds are empty. The only thing there is mind with nothing in it. This situation quickly changes. A two-year old is infamous for asking his mother question after question. She is there not just to feed and care for him, but to answer the questions that each unique child asks of her. Sometimes we suspect that this may be her most important motherly function. Chesterton said that the difference between a mother and a teacher is this: A teacher teaches a hundred children the same thing, while a mother must answer a hundred questions of one child.

Sometimes we reverse roles. Instead of a question seeking an answer, we say: "Now this is the answer, what is the question?" Obviously, answers do not just sit out there. An answer is a response to a question. The two belong together. Indeed, to recall Aquinas again, we do not understand the answer to any question unless we also understand the arguments against the truth as given to the question. An answer to a question is aware of other possible answers that are not true or only true in part.

If we go behind this question and answer business, we understand that the mind is made to function in this manner—step by step, one answer building on another. When we ask a question, we expect an answer. That is, we assume the world is so made that answers to our questions exist. It is our life's journey to find answers. So this journey includes asking the important questions, not that there is anything wrong with frivolous questions. Indeed, it may just be that what we once thought were frivolous questions turn out to lead us to the important answers.

One more curious aspect of questions and answers must be touched on here. While we do seek answers, we also are alert for answers that we suspect might be true but we do not want to hear them to be true because they would require us to do something about the answer as given. So what do we do? We invent a series of questions whose answers yield the results that we want, not the results that are true. This is what Plato meant about having a lie in our souls.

It turns out that not every answer to a question is true. There is no such thing as "my truth." There is only truth which I affirm or reject. If everyone has his own "truth," then none of us has any-thing in common. We cannot be friends. We cannot even live in the same universe. The denial that some answers are true ironically makes "every man an island." We are all floating about in our own universe with no way to make contact with one another.

The question is important because it generates an answer. But it is the answer and its truth that make any question worth asking, any life worth living.

Chapter 14
ON "CULTURE OF EVIL"

Several years ago in the *National Review*, Robert Reilly wrote a seminal essay entitled, "The Culture of Vice." (It can still be found through Google). I have often returned to this brief, remarkable essay. It explains better than almost anything I know what has happened to our recent culture and why.

Reilly begins the essay with the famous citation from Aristotle that men begin revolutions from motives stemming from their "private lives." Plato had long taught us that a disorder in soul, especially in the souls of the talented and attractive, would eventually, if not corrected, result in a disorder of polity.

Reilly explains how this happens. Essentially, evil and good change places both in custom and law. Evil still remains evil. Good remains good. That does not and cannot change. But we can pretend that the two can transform themselves into each other.

"Vice" is a technical term. It means a bad or evil way of life by which we habituate ourselves always to choose what is wrong over against what is right. Our freedom is such that we can do this switching. "Virtue" is the opposite of vice.

Habits whereby we usually choose what is right, but not always, Aristotle called "continent," and where we mostly choose what is wrong, but not always, "incontinent." He thought that most people most of the time fell into these two middle positions.

Aristotle, however, was aware of the probability of those who choose evil in their own souls to corrupt the rest of the society. This process of overturning good to call evil good is what Reilly means by the "culture of evil."

Essentially, this is the project that C. S. Lewis once pointed out of making what is evil to be good and what is good to be evil. This latter cannot in fact be done. But it can be made to appear that it can. Such is the power of persuasion, public opinion and positive law.

Reilly was concerned with how homosexuality and abortion came to be considered "rights" and "virtues." Both remained what they are, no matter what they are called or what the law states and enforces. That is, their corrupting effects will be manifest even though we refuse to recognize them.

What is brilliant about the Reilly essay, however, is the clear insight into the process by which what is originally seen to be a vice can, over time, come to be called a "virtue" or a "right." The main issue or move does not at first appear in the public order.

The general steps are these: The first step is sympathy. We do not recognize a natural law in things and especially human things whereby we know what these vices are. We plead sympathy for the one who practices them. If he refuses to change, repent, or seek forgiveness, he must come to hate a world that defines vice as vice. He turns on the world, not on his soul.

Everyone wants approval. The tolerance of the vice comes next. The vice is an exceptional case, but we overlook it. It is purely private. But it is what we want. We cannot accept the distinction between practice and tendency. We have a "right" to practice our vice. The word "right" is so fuzzy.

If we have a "right," nothing really can be wrong with our ways. Those who insist that something is wrong "discriminate." The law must guarantee our "right" to practice what we define as good. To do this "right," we must eliminate from the world any sign of intelligence whereby certain activities are wrong or unnatural.

We develop a theory of the cosmos to support our practice. It reveals nothing about what we are. Our freedom thus really means our "right" to fashion ourselves to be whatever kind of being we want. No standard of the human exists.

The final step makes what was once called virtue to be a vice. Moreover, the "vice" called "virtue" is embodied in the civil law with its coercive powers. No one can question the legitimacy of the vice-become-virtue. The whole structure of education, work, family, military, government, and religion must conform to the "new law" now normative for everyone.

When it is spelled out this way, we can see that such is pretty much the path that western civilization has followed in the recent past. The "private" vices have become public law imposed on everyone. It is all very logical as vice usually is. Reilly's description of the projection of our inner vices onto the culture is gripping.

What is provocative about Reilly's analysis is the realization that no one can simply live with his own sins if he chooses not to acknowledge what they are. He must insist that his sins be recognized as good. Christianity has long suspected that purely "private" sins do not exist. Reilly's essay tells us why. It is, as I say, a remarkable essay.

Chapter 15
ON THE EMPTY UNIVERSE

Our cosmos, our universe, is said to be devoid of meaning, that is, of a reason why it is as it is. This "lack of cosmic order" thesis has ulterior motives lurking in its advocate's mind. We have, it is said, developed elaborate creation "myths" about the origins and apparent order of things. Such theories of an ordered universe are but intellectual "super-structures" with no foundations in things.

Those who claim that a God is needed to explain what order seems to be there are merely projecting their desires onto things. The mind, when it examines the world, finds nothing there except chance and more chance. Since chance could be otherwise at every instant, nothing is really out there to be found. Nothing has ever happened. Nothing "caused" something else to take place. Just how, by this same chance, a "mind" came about that could "see" that no order existed is something of a puzzle.

At first sight, this empty universe view seems exhilarating. Many think it to be the basis of "humanism." If nothing is found "out there," then human beings are "free." No law or *logos* exists to hamper us. We are beholden to nothing but ourselves. Our nobility lies in imposing our ideas, whatever they are, on a "meaning-less" reality. Our wills, not our intelligence, define reality.

But since we obviously do not all have the same ideas, we have no criteria but power for judging which idea is better than another. We must, evidently, allow for even contradictory ideas lest we raise the unsettling question of why one idea is "better" than another. Yet, recurring stabilities appear in the universe. Our human nature seems to be one of them. If what we call our human nature were, at bottom, itself a constantly changing chance, we must conclude that we ourselves really do not exist. This alternative seems for

}51{

many preferable to one holding that man knows a reality and is responsible for what he finds there.

In Colossians, after stating that Christ is "the image of the invisible God," Paul added that He "is before all that is." Thus, *all that* is does not just sit there as if it were related to nothing but itself. The universe did not sound so empty to Paul. But he recognized that man did claim to be unable to see God's order in the world. How did Paul explain this situation? "You yourselves were once alienated from him (Christ); you nourished hostility in your hearts because of your evil deeds" (1:15, 21). That memorable passage suggests that theories implying an empty universe do not really arise from experience or science. They arise rather in order to make "evil deeds" seem normal and permissible. Thus, we have no desire to confront them or change them. What we do is what we want to do, not what we ought to do.

It is too facile to propose that behind every aberrant intellectual theory, especially those that presuppose an empty universe, lay a moral problem in the soul of its advocate. But I suspect that it is true in the vast majority of the cases. Something curious goes on here. I have often been struck by the phrase in the Canticle of Zechariah that asks the Lord to "free us from the hands of all those who hate us" (Luke 1: 71). In some sense, the empty universe is the result of hatred for a universe of meaning and order that finds its origin in a *Logos*, in a God who is the truth. The burden of much of modern thought is precisely to rid the universe of the vestiges of God. God is hated because He expects us to use our intelligence and good sense to live an ordered, even noble life. The problem is not that we often try and fail. That is the realm of forgiveness. We recognize our need of God when we acknowledge our need of forgiveness. But if we can do nothing wrong, forgiveness is beside the point.

Lucifer was one of the most brilliant of the angels. His "fall," from all we can tell, had to do with his refusal to accept the order that God had set in the world. His fall did not mean that he lost his intelligence. It meant that he used his intelligence to foil the plans of God as it existed in the souls of men. Those who want to empty the universe of all order do so because they want to eliminate the possibility of anyone finding God in His creation. What they are left with is their own freedom. That is all. It is called hell in other contexts. In the end, the empty universe leaves us only looking at ourselves, to the exclusion of the wonders of a creation whose gift to us is not just ourselves but everything else *that is*.

Chapter 16
On My "Right" to Everything

We can approach political things from two angles: "What ought I to do?" or "What is owed to me?" The first approach requires that we acquire sufficient virtue to rule ourselves to do what objectively is worth doing. The second approach looks to someone else to supply what we cannot obtain or make for ourselves.

These alternatives occurred while watching several years ago the riotous reaction to the Greek austerity legislation. In our recent election the same issues appeared. We do not rely on ourselves but on someone else to provide what we want. Such a principle is quickly politicized into the notion that the government is responsible for me and everyone else. Thus, government defines my "rights" as measures of what it thinks man is. In lieu of higher law or reason, it brooks in practice no other source but itself as the origin of "rights."

Unfortunately, many governments delight in conceiving themselves as the responsible organ for caring for everything and everyone. The more people depend on the government, the more secure it is in its own power and longevity. What is the origin of this citizen willingness to cede to the government the responsibility for defining and supplying our "rights?" Several components are pertinent.

The first source is Hobbes on "rights." Every individual has a "right" to everything he wants and needs. Of course, this situation can produce a nasty conflict. We come to blows when we all want the same scarce things. We fight it out. This "war of all against all" just makes things worse. Finally, we agree to appoint someone stronger than we who will prevent our mutual clashes for what we need.

Since we all fear "violent" death, we empower the state to define and arrange what we receive. Theoretically, this mechanism leaves us in peace to produce more of the goods that we need. The all-powerful state convinces itself that it can take care of everyone by neutralizing each person's or group's power to obtain whatever he wants. We replace it with whatever the state will give. The "cost" is that we cannot "hold" our own ideas and beliefs. They are the real causes of our struggles with one another. The price of peace is state control of ideas and religion.

The second origin of "rights" is a secularized version of Christianity. We hear of "preferential options for the poor." Government is to be a "servant" of all. Charity deals with cases that society cannot handle. Everyone is concerned with everyone else. But next we notice that ideas of caring for the poor, of service, and of charity gradually are subsumed by institutions of the state, which is pleased to have them. Even Christians begin to talk primarily of what the government must do for this or that segment of the population that cannot or will not care for itself.

Religious institutions become directly or indirectly financed by the state. It has its own rules for the uses of its monies. People have a "right" to such things. Once they know that they have a "right," they put two and two together. They look at the state to supply their "rights." Few care about how to supply what is demanded. They still "demand" them. The state thus understands itself as a mortal god, a supplier of "rights." A certain almost mystical exhilaration is found in taking care of others, even all others.

We try to balance these positions with "duty." No "rights" can exist without corresponding "duties." One problem with this approach is the Kantian notion of "duties." If we ask, "Why are you helping me out?" and the answer is that "It is my 'duty,'" we feel it has little to do with us. One is only dealing with himself and his "duties."

What is missing in all of this rights-virtue-duties talk? It is not freedom, which could be part of the problem. If freedom is the pursuit of whatever we want, which was, for Aristotle, the formal element of a "democratic" form of government, we soon discover that we want everything. We insist that we have a "right" to it. By looking at what is owed to us, we become oblivious to what we need to do to provide for ourselves. We understand the common good as a distributive justice in which the state provides everything for us.

We need conceptions of rights, virtue, duties, and freedom that enable us to care for ourselves. We need a conception of a limited state, whose purpose is not to do everything itself but to recognize arenas of responsibility in which individuals and groups are the main source of providing for themselves. The democratic, all-caring state provides all our "rights," however we define them. Such is the polity that has emerged from the souls of our citizens' freedom. My "right" to everything is not a pretty sight.

Chapter 17
ON PHILOSOPHICAL EROS

In book seven of the *Republic*, Socrates asks: "What then, Glaucon, would be a study to draw the soul from becoming to being?" (521d). This question we do not ask ourselves every day, though perhaps we should. The question inquires about a "study" that might incite us to consider things of highest importance. We do not automatically make this step by ourselves. Many of us need to be awakened, even prodded. We need to be "turned around," as Socrates tells us. Yet, we all have in us the capacity to know. Indeed, more than anything else, this capacity defines us. We are the beings who by nature seek to know, know *what is*, whatever it is.

Later in this same book, we read: "For souls, you know, are far more likely to be cowardly in severe [difficult] studies than in gymnastics. The labor is closer to home in that it is the soul's privately, and not shared in common with the body" (535b). That is, though both are important, sports are easier to comprehend than metaphysics. Yet, sports too can wake us up to notice the existence of things worthy in themselves.

When we read this passage about cowardly souls, we remember that this same Glaucon was called "brave" by Socrates in the second book because he insisted on asking Socrates about the truth even when he could make persuasive arguments for its impossibility. The military virtue, bravery, came to be applied to philosophical inquiry, to the insistence on knowing the truth, nothing less.

No doubt few things are more needed today than our courage to ask about the truth of the reigning moral aberrations now increasingly established as law and custom by our regime and with the consent of most of us. In a world where relativism is king, truth finds itself the martyr. Where truth cannot be spoken, no one can reform his life.

How is this issue understood? Our courts and university faculties are no longer courageous enough to ask whether what they were deciding and teaching is true. In order to avoid this basic question—"Is it true?"—with an answer not merely an opinion, they have preferred to go on and on making distinctions and equivocations that would allow them to continue to undermine our moral and intellectual stature so that they could justify certain ways of acting and living.

The term "philosophical *eros*" comes from the followers of Leo Strauss. It refers to Socrates, of course. At first sight, to juxtapose "*eros*" and philosophy is just as odd as to juxtapose courage and philosophic inquiry. We assume that "*eros*" and philosophy oppose each other or are about different things. Plato himself implied this difference in the famous fifth book of the *Republic*. "Eros," as it were, is a bodily word; philosophy is a heady one. Yet, the phrase, "philosophical *eros*," intrigues us. Ideas will not let us alone.

The term "philosophical *Eros*" means, roughly, that we should pursue the truth with the same passion and zeal that we pursue our beloved. Indeed, it implies, at least in Christianity, that we can, if we will, pursue the truth even if we give up the normal consummation of *eros* in marriage. But philosophical *eros* and marriage are not in conflict either, except perhaps in St. Paul's sense that the married man has many concerns.

We live in a time when any notion that truth exists or that it should be pursued is identified with fanaticism. The skeptic will fanatically pursue his own skepticism, while those who pursue the truth he will call "fanatics." And while the principle of non-contradiction remains the fundamental philosophical tool, we find that it means little to those who do not mind giving their souls to contradiction in order that they do not have to acknowledge error and change their ways.

Augustine, in a famous passage, told us that two loves built two cities. He meant that it is quite possible to pursue falsity and evil, claiming it to be good, with every bit as much passion as the saints pursue the truth. *"Eros,"* as such, in other words, what is simply bodily, is not itself the last criterion of truth. The martyr is indeed a witness who suffers for his cause, but if he is not a witness to truth, he is doubly dangerous.

The world, we can say, is in some sense built on ideas. If the ideas are wrong, the structure of the human world will be wrong. We do not like to admit that our "subjective" ideas have "consequences." We like to think, with the Supreme Court, that we can construct our own vision of reality that has no need to inquire whether it is true or not. In such a world, we cannot even talk to one another nor have any issue between us resolved by persuasion. Philosophical *eros* does not let us rest with such illusory opinions in our souls.

Chapter 18
ON WHAT IF TRUTH DIDN'T MATTER?

I have always loved the title of Christopher Derrick's little book on Thomas Aquinas College *Escape from Scepticism: Liberal Education as if the Truth Really Mattered*. It is a book the late Thomas Dillon wanted to keep in print. As I think about that title now, I like to pose to myself the opposite question: "What if the truth does not matter?" What follows?

Strictly speaking, of course, if there is no truth, nothing follows. The very idea that something follows from something else implies that there is an order both in the mind and in things and they are related. Truth means that our minds are conformed to *what is*. Descartes, following a famous passage in Augustine, affirmed that if "I" doubt everything, I must be there someplace, since I know that it is "I" who doubts everything. To "doubt" is to look ourselves in the eyes and ask, "Pardon me, but who are you?"

What is this "I" who doubts? How did it get there? Or at least the "I" with which Schall is most familiar knows he did not get there out of himself. And if I doubt, I must already have some idea of what it is not to doubt. I cannot have one without the other. I always love the image of the person who goes about wondering whether he exists, while, at the same time, saying "excuse me" after he steps on some one's toe or spills a glass of wine while dining at guests.

In Leszek Kolakowski's most useful book, *Why Is There Something Rather than Nothing?*, the last sentence in the chapter on the great Sceptic, Sextus Empiricus, reads: "Does the Sceptic contradict himself in expounding the Sceptical doctrine? Should he not rather remain silent, if he is to be consistent?" The answer to that question is, of course, "yes." And it is an ancient answer as well as a present one. Why on earth would someone who really doubts everything try to convince Schall that he doubts both of their existences?

The current rush to study Muslim philosophy, with its reference to Allah as unlimited will, is but another form of this same background. In another form, it was called "Occasionalism." This meant that nobody really did anything. No secondary causes existed, only the First Cause. To maintain that Schall ever "did" something (which can be doubted!) implied a mistrust of God's power. To praise God we had to say that nothing else did anything, including Schall. God did everything.

In this sense, the Sceptic and the fideist believer agreed about the world. Behind the world there was either nothing or Something, but there was no bridge from my doubt that I am to the nothing or the Something that may or may not be out there. In either case, we have a "faith" with no grounding, with no reason.

In a famous passage in his *Closing of the American Mind*, Allan Bloom said that every professor, when he enters a classroom, can presume that every student before him is either a relativist or claims he is one. The relativist who just "claims" that he is one, however, still opens the door before entering the classroom. Such relativism is indeed but a form of Scepticism.

Derrick's book begins with the premise that Scepticism contradicts itself. That is, in its very statement of itself, it affirms what it denies. Once we see that, we can go cheerfully to other truths that also matter. The very title of Kolakowski's book, which comes at least from Leibnitz, is a good next question. Eric Voegelin loved this question also. We pretty quickly notice that we are a something, a this thing, not that thing. We find it difficult to imagine a "nothing" happily engaged in conversation with another "nothing," though Belloc is said to have loved a famous novel entitled, *The Diary of a Nobody*. A "Nobody" who writes a diary is a "Somebody."

In Aquinas' famous Disputed Question on Truth, he warns against "frivolous multiplication" of questions. That could lead to infinity, which would make the whole process of truth finding "in vain," that is, hopeless. He then goes on to cite a brief sentence from Aristotle's *Metaphysics*: "We define the truth as 'to say that what *is* is and that what is not *is* not." Such lines, not unsurprisingly, are also found in Plato's *Republic*.

Today, it takes courage to say that there is truth. Derrick was struck by a college that built "liberal education" on this very premise. In fact, it is difficult to see on what other premise one could build a college and still have what is, in effect, either "liberal" or an "education."

What we now call "multiculturalism," "historicism," "diversity," "positivism," "hate language," even "theoretic tolerance," are, on examining how they are mostly used, really euphemisms for Scepticism or relativism. With such an education based on these principles, we have no idea who or what we are, which seems like an odd purpose for education of any sort.

How are we to live in such a world? A backward glance may help. On July 20, 1762, Samuel Johnson wrote from London to Joseph Baretti in Milan. Johnson had just taken a nostalgic trip back to his home town in Litchfield. He found the local streets "narrower" and "shorter," than he remembered them.

A new "race of people" lived there whom he did not recognize. His "playfellows" were now "grown old," which led him to suspect that he too "was no longer young." He did run into a "remaining friend" from his youth, but found, in a provocative phrase, that the friend had "changed his principles."

Johnson's step-daughter was still there. He had expected much of her and greeted her with "sincere benevolence." However, she had lost the "beauty and gaiety of youth" but did not "gain much of the wisdom of age." He wandered about his home town for about five days.

The whole experience so annoyed Johnson that he took the first "convenience" back to London. He described this city, most profoundly, really, "as a place where, if there is not much happiness, there is at least such diversity of good and evil that slight vexations do not fix upon the heart" (*Samuel Johnson: The Major Works*, Penguin, 85).

Why do I cite Johnson here? At close quarters, "slight vexations" do "fix upon the heart." Little things become big ones. We need to be fixed upon the great questions: "Why is there something rather than nothing?" "What is truth?" Indeed, much happiness is not found in the big city. We cannot doubt what is before our very eyes. That too is a question of "liberal education," namely, "Why the city?"

And yes, that "diversity of good and evil"—Nietzsche, in the next century, will tell us that he is well "beyond" it. The Sceptics of our time, no doubt, assure us that no standard for this distinction exists. We read our Machiavelli. What pleases the "prince" or the "prophet"? What he says about life and happiness is "the law."

It is the grand "vexations" that should "fix our hearts." This is the truth that really matters. This is the education that is "freeing," that is, "liberal."

The most famous question about truth in the New Testament was asked by a politician. It was: "What is truth?" The most famous statement about liberal education in the same New Testament concerned what would "free" us. The answer was "truth." It was spoken by the very man to whom the politician spoke.

We could not tell of the "diversity of good and evil" among us in the big cities if what is good and what is evil changed every day, or if each was what the politician decided it to be. A Sceptic cannot, in logic, distinguish between good and evil. Ultimately, he too is reduced to silence. We do whatever we want but cannot talk about it.

Johnson found cities to be places where the large questions were before us, whether we like it or not. What would it "matter" if truth didn't matter? We cannot even pose the question as if its answer did not matter. And this brings us back to Aristotle, to the root of liberal education, which, if we are fortunate, we can find being taught here and there.

"Truth is to say of *what is* that it *is*, and of what is not, that it is not." That is the affirmation that "really matters." Never doubt it.

Chapter 19
ON SAVING "THE PEOPLE FROM THEIR SINS"

While staying in the rectory of the St. Thomas Aquinas Newman Club at the University of North Dakota, on the shelves of the guest room I noticed the B.A.C. edition of Aquinas' *Summa Theologiae*. I had seen this edition before.

With a few moments to spare, I took down the Third Part of the *Summa*, the volume devoted to Christ. This third part has a brief Prologue explaining its purpose. Unless we pay attention, the very structure of the *Summa* will seem strange to us. How to put it? In the first question that follows this Prologue, Aquinas asks not "Whether the Incarnation was necessary?" but whether it was "convenient"? If it was merely "convenient," but not "necessary," then the Incarnation did not need to happen. If it did not "need" to happen, but did happen, then we must wonder why it happened in terms other than necessity.

What does this "did not need to happen" mean? Evidently, it means that God could have redeemed the human race in a way other than through the Incarnation of one of the Persons of the Trinity, the Word, the Son. The import of Aquinas' question then is clearly, "Why was it done this way, through the Incarnation?" That is, can we, stimulated by the fact of the Incarnation, find a reason for it that makes sense, perhaps the highest sense? Still, it must be a reason that does not make this Incarnation "necessary," as if God were determined to use this way and no other. This restriction leads us to wonder what is higher than "necessity?"

In an essay on the structure of the *Summa*, the great Dominican theologian, M-D Chenu, wrote:

> The vision of God is realized only by and in Christ. Still, to Saint Thomas' way of thinking, our knowledge of

God must be examined first in its own inner structure and demands before we can appreciate all the precious and manifold Christ-like ways in which it may manifest itself. The Word, made flesh for our ransoming, is the heart and soul, so to say, of the economy of our Christian redemption; yet the basic source of the understandableness of this economy (to minds such as ours, at any rate) is precisely its property of being a *via* or means. To see it thus inserted within the ontological framework of grace is not to lessen its inestimable value as a fact of history, unfolding in time (*Thomist Reader*, 1958).

What this explanation implies is that our philosophical and theological understanding of God does not tell us what God, as a free and personal being, will do in an actual world that He created but did not need to create. He will achieve His purposes in His own way in dealing with creatures who are really free, that is, with us.

Thus, to return to Aquinas' Prologue, he begins by citing the passage of the Angel in Matthew (1:24). Christ came to "Save His people from their sins." So we begin with a factual historical situation from Genesis. The actual existing race of men whom Christ came to save has a history in which men are mired because of their sins. This is a fact. They need a "way" out of their lot that they cannot achieve or imagine by their own powers, individual or collective. Yet, they still know by natural reasoning even before Christ's Incarnation what is right and wrong. But they cannot seem to practice it. What they need is precisely a divine response to their situation, one that respects the freedom of both man and God.

Christ first demonstrates to us that the way of truth is Himself, the point Benedict make in *Jesus of Nazareth*. Through His rising again to immortal life, we are able to perceive the significance of the whole theological enterprise. But we can do this only after having first considered what we can know with our human reason about the ultimate end of human life and of the virtues and vices. This consideration was the subject of the earlier two books of the *Summa*. With this background, we can consider and seek to understand as much as we can of this very Savior and His benefices to the human race.

We thus first consider what the Savior is, then the sacraments by which salvation is attained, and finally the end of immortal life to which, through this very resurrection, we arrive. Since the purpose of the Savior coming is "to save the people from their sins," the structure of the Incarnation, as it were, takes places through the consequences of these sins. The way that God in His Trinitarian reasoning decides to save us is not through power or necessity, but through our freedom and the divine freedom.

Aquinas' question was: "Whether it was 'convenient' that we were redeemed in a peculiar way, through the Incarnation, life and death of the God-man?" It need not have happened this way. What was the *via*, the way, in which it did happen? We were shown the consequences of our sins by this God-man who is Christ suffering for us. We remain free to accept or reject this way. It is a way that is in conformity with the highest in us and in God. It is a way that does not "force" us to be free, but one that invites us to be free. The initiative of God in the Incarnation and Redemption stems from something beyond justice and necessity. It is the intervention of a love for us that does not seek to save us by overpowering us. Rather on seeing the consequences of our sins in Christ's suffering, it invites us to understand and choose. It is, indeed, a most "convenient" way.

Chapter 20

ON JUSTICE

Benedict XVI associated justice with judgment. In speaking of justice, we acknowledge injustice's possibility. We cannot talk of either justice or injustice without talking of judgment. Injustice, to recall, "cries out." Judgment is unpopular today. It implies a standard that we do not make but to which, to be reasonable, we are to adhere.

Concern about justice has Platonic overtones. Was the world created in justice? It doesn't seem so. If not, the world cannot be coherent. Likewise, in all existing cities, in all times and places, many crimes and violations of justice go unpunished; many noble deeds go unrequited. This situation is difficult to square with a just God or universe. Both in Plato and in revelation, we find a final judgment. This judgment is not an accident.

No human being is simply a product of chance. Each person has origins in the vast creative potential within the Godhead. This fact does not mean that no element of chance is found in our individual lives. But chance itself is the result of the crossing of voluntary and necessary acts. From our viewpoint, what looks like chance looks like purpose within a providential order.

The most significant entities in creation are not stars, planets, comets, black holes, or other sidereal phenomena. They exist from the ages in order that within the universe a creature might exist which is directly intended by God for Himself. The order of cosmic development is anthropic in character. Once the cosmos itself exists, with the sundry orders of living and sentient beings within it, we only begin the drama of what the universe is about.

The human being is the one being in the physical cosmos which belongs both to the world and to what transcends the world. All levels of being are found within each human person—

mineral, vegetable, animal, spirit. They exist there in a coherent whole.

Every human being, however, finds that he does not just live in a physical world. He lives in a world of pleasures and pains, of opinions, thoughts, willings, and searchings. His own good is not simply himself. He exists "for himself" in order that he may act, know, and choose. To be what he is, it is not enough simply to be.

With some experience, we learn that we can make ourselves into what we ought not to be. When we make such wrong turns, we wonder if we can straighten things out. Yet, we may not want to change. We do not want to be bothered by any comparing of ourselves with what we ought to be. We can harden our hearts.

Alongside the "empirical" world, we find another world, related to it, but one existing because words and actions have been placed in the world through human beings acting for some end or purpose. This world is the "social" or "moral" world. Within it we find realities such as anger, love, hatred, piety, honor, stealing, murder, cheating, gift-giving, with all sorts of things that arise in their source from the rational creature.

The human being is itself an order of parts to whole and of whole to end. He has a certain autonomy. This autonomy enable him to become what he ought to be, or, conversely, to reject it. We are responsible for ourselves and for one another. Familial and civil orders are intended to assist us to be what we ought to be, though they can also guide us in the opposite direction. They too are not independent of what-it-is-to-be-human. They do not make man to be man, as Aristotle said, but are designed to assist him in being good man.

Why would a pope who often speaks of charity and generosity spend time on justice? Here I do not mean the dubious notion of "social justice," the origins of which imply intellectual efforts to place man's transcendent end in his own hands to be achieved in this world by his own powers.

The justice that deals with judgment looks soberly at the human condition. We live in a save-everybody-world or, conversely, in a world in which nothing is worth saving. Christianity transcends the polities. It is not unaware of what goes on in them.

Plato warned us that the greatest crimes against the human person often came from politicians seeking honor. Hannah Arendt indicated that even insignificant persons can commit great crimes. The combination of justice and judgment arises here.

Even if we are praised for it, not all we do is right. Justice is present. Our deeds will be judged. We can avail ourselves of punishment, forgiveness, and charity. If we do not, and we need not, what is left is transcendent judgment in justice. The papal reminder reaches the very depths of our contemporary being. We choose not to notice.

Chapter 21

ON LOS GATOS

Many people know that Schall retired after the Fall Semester (2012) at Georgetown University. In March, he moved to the Jesuit Center in Los Gatos, California. Before departing, saying good-bye to friends, a letter from the university provost informed him that he was now a "Professor Emeritus." It is a rite of passage. One's official status is "old age." Cicero, in his essay, "On Old Age,"," spoke about the "activities" of old age. The old themselves usually include their aches and pains. Most cultures associate old age with wisdom, though the expression "an old fool" is not unheard of.

On the first day of spring, I boarded an Alaska Airline plane to San Jose via Los Angeles. At LAX, I had to go from one terminal to another, something this airport makes most difficult to do. Fortunately, a fellow Jesuit, Kevin O'Brien, was on the same plane and negotiated me through the terminals.

When the plane to San Jose was ready to take off, the pilot told us that a small "problem" in the tail needed checking—only ten minutes. Two hours later, with a different plane and crew, we took off for San Jose, the nearest airport to Los Gatos. I stayed over the weekend with a nephew who lives twenty miles from Los Gatos. He delivered me to the new house on Monday morning.

I had lived in this house as a novice. In fact, the room I am currently occupying is right across the aisle from the one I had as a novice in 1948—a visible Alpha and Omega situation. This house has about seventy men in it, many old classmates, now retired. Some are in the infirmary. The staff is most helpful. It took about a week to settle in, get used to a routine.

This property is about one hundred and eighty acres, on a hillside overlooking the lovely town of Los Gatos and the majestic

Santa Clara Valley. Hiking trails wend back of us up the mountain. This is spring. Everything is green. Flowers are everywhere. Temperature is mild. The gardens around the house are very nice. The city of San Jose is clear in the distance, as is the Mt. Hamilton Range across the Valley. We are in the foothills of the Santa Cruz Mountains which separate the San Francisco Bay from the Ocean at Santa Cruz.

This house was founded by the Jesuits from the Turin Province back in the late 1800's. Naturally, they brought the vine and the olive with them. In my younger years, Novitiate of Los Gatos wines were quite well known. But the winery has long closed though its buildings are now operated by the "Testarossa" Winery.

On the pasture above the house are five jackasses. They are pets, though their forefathers once ploughed the vines on the hillsides above the house. A donkey is a domesticated jackass. A jack is a male ass. I will presume that readers know what a mule or a hinny is, how each is related to horses and donkeys.

In any case, as I was walking down the hill the other day, the five jackasses in the pasture followed me to their feed lot, evidently thinking that I had an apple for them. Needless to say, this image of Schall being followed by five jackasses is open to considerable pious interpretation on the part of the brethren.

The main topic of conversation around here is the new pope. Fortunately, my copies of *L'Osservatore Romano* have been arriving. I have been able to read what Pope Francis has been doing and saying. In one homily, he told priests that they should be out in the world—preaching, baptizing, consoling, and not sitting around like bureaucrats and psychoanalyzing themselves.

When the pope told his relatives and friends in Argentina not to come to his inaugural ceremonies but to stay at home and give the travel money to the poor, I thought: "There went the Italian tourist industry!" I wondered just who the poor were who would receive this unspent Argentine money. How much would it actually help them without a productive economic system?

Of late, I have been thinking that we have turned almost every help giving agency over to the state. Helping the poor now means, not working for a living, but setting up another state care program. Most states are delighted to oblige. They more and more forbid any spontaneous or non-government help. The state wants the poor as a reason to justify its, the state's, existence and expansion. I fear the term "social justice" usually means, in practice, something like expanding this state control.

So Schall can find things to think about in Los Gatos. It is not Washington. But the shadow of Washington is here. Retired priests too can find something to do. Benedict, the pope, set the example.

Chapter 22

ON THE "UNEQUAL DISTRIBUTION OF GOODS"

On January 25 at St. Paul's Outside the Walls Basilica, the Holy Father spoke of the ecumenical movement. He recalled the differences that still exist among Christians, a scandalous division. Benedict commemorated the 1910 Edinburgh World Council of Churches meeting. It first called attention to the negative effect of this division in the missions. All Christians, however, agree on some issues. About certain broad issues of humanity, everyone, Christian or not, can agree. The final listed common issue is "the unequal distribution of goods."

This latter expression occurs frequently in papal and religious documents. Mr. Obama has espoused this wording. I frankly wonder what exactly it means. Clearly, the world's "goods" will never be "equally" distributed nor would we want them to be. Obviously, the expression "equally" cannot be taken literally.

One might say that we look to the "proportionate" distribution of goods. But if this is what we mean, why cannot we just say that? Proportionate does not mean equal, except in the case of distributive justice where it logically means that to be equal things must be unequal. Those who contribute more deserve more.

Most utopian ideologies, perhaps following Plato's "communality of property," have proposed a version of this "equal distribution" as a solution to men's problems. Aristotle examines the shortcomings of such notions in the second book of his *Politics*.

If things are not "equally distributed," who can devise a plan to right this wrong? The state? The United Nations? On what grounds? Do we follow Robin Hood: Take from the rich and give it to the poor? Will Robin Hood be just? Will the state? The UN? Who will watch the watchdogs? Machiavelli says that men are more likely to forgive you for murdering your father than for taking their goods.

One issue immediately arises: How were the goods we distribute "equally" produced in the first place? Does everyone create wealth "equally"? Are the talent and discipline necessary to produce wealth itself equally distributed? If we do not reward more those who produce wealth, will they do much to continue to produce it? Or is everything to be done altruistically? "To each according to his capacity, to all according to his needs?" as Marx said.

"Redistribution" assumes that the world is narrowly limited. We hear overtones of a static earth, of a finite sum of goods unrelated to human enterprise. Sometimes, the ideal is: "Do nothing so that the world can be passed on untouched to every generation down the ages." Human beings consume irreplaceable resources. Obviously, the admonition of Genesis means that the world and its riches are for man.

But these "riches" must be discovered and developed. Wealth, needed for human living, arises not from goods themselves but from the human mind as it learns how to produce what is needed by our kind. We did not always know such means.

St Paul stated: "We used to lay down the rule that anyone who would not work should not eat.... We urge the strong in the Lord Jesus Christ to earn the food they eat by working quietly" (2 Thess. 3). If we assume that the world's goods are "ill-distributed," must the sole cause be those who have learned to produce wealth? Do our economic, moral, religious, or political systems or our virtues and vices have anything to do with it? If so, can any "redistribution" occur without a change in these areas?

Moreover, not everyone wants to be wealthy. Some want to be wealthy but do not want to work to achieve it, or do not know how to achieve it. Some belong to a government, religion, or ideology that, even at its best, will not achieve it, will not work.

It is said that if we take any population and arbitrarily allot to each an equal amount of goods, that, in a few years of exchange, the same pattern of unequal distribution will recur. Why? Not all people go to the trouble of working to keep their property. Too, there is still vice. Not everyone works well.

Aristotle, as he so often did, had it mostly right. "The wickedness of human beings is insatiable," he said.

> At first the two obol allowance (minimum wage) was adequate, but now that this is something traditional, they always ask for more, and go on doing so without limit. For the nature of desire is without limit, and it is with a view to satisfying this that many live. To rule such persons, then, requires not so much leveling property as providing that those who are moderate by nature will be the sort who have no wish to aggrandize themselves... (1267b1–6).

In other words, I would like to hear the last of the "redistribution of goods" talk as if it were something either possible or desirable without so many qualifications that the phrase, as an obvious proposal, becomes meaningless.

Chapter 23

ON INTELLIGENCE

A year previous to his cardinalate (1969), Jean Daniélou entitled a booklet, *La crise actuelle de l'intelligence*. These years saw social and political turmoil. Daniélou wished to comprehend them. The root of this crisis is found in the mind, in how we philosophically understood ourselves in the world. He agreed with the classics that lives lacking virtue exist. They exercise a major influence on how the will allows the mind to see its proper object, namely, *what is*.

The dominant way to "understand" anything today is "science." That is, by the use of hypotheses, testing, logic, reconsidering, and rigorous care of detail. In his Bradley Lecture, Harvey Mansfield remarked: "To scientists, the university is divided into science and non-science; the latter is not knowledge and is likely to be mush (in which they are right). Scientists easily forget that science cannot prove science is good, that their whole project is founded upon what is at best unscientific common sense. They do not see that the unscientific foundation of science leaves science far short of wisdom, whether practical or theoretical." The first part of the Daniélou essay said the same thing.

Visiting a number of universities at the time, including Berkeley, Daniélou observed that "these students do not come to the university to be debauched; they come essentially to be among intellectuals. They come to the university more to be able to discuss the great problems that are actually those of politics, of morals, and of man." What they find, however, is "science." Something is lacking. Souls are not filled.

Daniélou's analysis is rooted in Aquinas and Aristotle. Intelligence is broader than calculation or "reasoning." Studies of college graduates today show that they go through college and emerge without much power of "critical thinking." But this lack is usually just another word for scientific method.

Daniélou recalls that most of the important things we need to know cannot be learned by such scientific thinking. "Science cannot by itself explain man, and which for us is a basic issue, the relation between persons. I mean finally that what is most important for me is to know that which certain others basically think of themselves." E. F. Schumacher remarked, in *A Guide for the Perplexed*, that the most dangerous man in any society is the man who does not know himself." This self-knowledge is not "scientific."

"Basically, that which is essential for me," Daniélou continued, "is to be able to penetrate into the heart of others. It is at bottom that exchange by which heart is open to heart, that exchange which attains its summit in love, which exists in friendship but which exists also in interior communication at all levels." We see much of this view, of course, in Plato and Aristotle, Augustine and Aquinas. Benedict's *Deus Caritas Est* is to be included here also.

The human intelligence has naturally two ways of knowing. One is the calculating way, science at its best. But there is also intuition, the mind's capacity itself to see into the higher things. The higher things that we know, that our mother loves us, are not "reasoned" but they are known with a certainty that matches any scientific truth, which itself, of course, is always subject to revision.

This is what trust is all about. "The problem of authority is not fundamentally a problem of power, but a problem of confidence." This is why belief in God can be certain. We can trust testimony and experience, even when we make every effort to examine it with our rational approach. "Faith is essentially a question of confidence in a competence," Daniélou explains. The problem of faith is ultimately to know whether Jesus Christ appeared to us as competent in what concerns a domain which is that of his proper field: in knowledge of the Father."

In an essay in the *New York Times*, (May 14, 2011), we read that studies show little increase in quality of learning proportional to increased costs of administration and tuition. "The situation reflects a large cultural change in the relationship between students and colleges. The authority of educators has diminished, and the students are increasingly thought of by themselves and their colleges, as 'clients' or 'consumers'." This was the same point Daniélou made in 1968.

"Intelligence has consequences and weighs on the destiny of humanity," Daniélou concludes in a remarkable phrase. We underestimate ourselves if we maintain that thinking itself in its broadest scope is not vital to our civilization. We cannot neglect the full perfection of mind that is thinking of what is true. Yet, when we will not direct ourselves to what the mind intuits, we use our wills to direct our minds to theories and ideologies that explain not reality, but what will allow us to do what we want.

Chapter 24
ON THE "RIGHT" TO HAPPINESS

An amusing citation from Margaret Thatcher reads: "The problem with socialism is that you eventually run out of other people's money." The socialists, however, were not the only ones who would run out of other people's money. Democracies are quite capable of duplicating this feat.

The question is: "What entitles us to acquire other people's money in the first place?" Do other people have no money that is not ours if we "need" it? "Taxation," with or without representation, is about this issue. Who decides what we "need?" Who gets what is taken from us? On what grounds do they "deserve" it?

C. S. Lewis said that no one has a "right" to happiness. Our Declaration only says that we have a "right" to "pursue" it. Whether we attain it is not something that falls under the perplexing language of "rights." If someone else "guarantees" my "right" to be "happy," what am I? Surely not a human being, whose happiness, as Aristotle said, includes an individual's own activity, not someone else's.

In a world of "rights," no one can give anything to anybody else. Everything is "owed" to me if I do not already have it. If I am not happy, I am a "victim" of someone else's negligence. A "rights-society" is litigious. If I am unhappy, it has nothing to do with me, with my own choices or habits. My "unhappiness" is caused by someone else who has violated my "rights."

Unhappy people presume that the violation of their "rights" is always caused by someone else. Their unhappiness does not involve them. Their mode is not "What can I do for others?" but "What must they do for me to make me happy?"

In his *Ethics*, Aristotle remarked that, if happiness were a gift of the gods, surely they would give it to us. No Christian can read such a line without pause. Is not the whole essence of our faith that we have no "right" either to existence itself or to a happy existence? Some things must first be given to us, no doubt, including our very selves, which we do not cause.

Indeed, the whole essence of revelation is that we do not have a "right" to the "eternal life" that God has promised to us. We cannot achieve it by ourselves because it is not a product of our own making or thinking. God does not violate our "rights" by not giving us either existence or happiness. Creation is not an act of justice.

The doctrine of grace opposes the notion that we have a "right" to happiness. It is not even something that we "deserve" or can "work for." At first sight, this primacy of gift and grace seems to lessen our dignity which, surely, ought to include some input on our part.

Christianity says that indeed this givenness is the case. We are given what we have no "right" to receive. This "givenness" should make us like the Giver, should incite us to something more than our own "rights." Happiness evidently lies beyond "rights." We can only speak of a "right" to happiness with many distinctions.

What was the point of Margaret Thatcher's quip about running out of someone else's money? Some do demand someone else's money. From whence does this "demand" arise? From those who claim that they have a "right" to happiness. If they do not have what others have, it is a sign, not of one's own failure to embrace the habits and ways to produce what is needed, but of someone unjustly having what I think I need. Thus, I do not have to earn what I need. The mere fact that I do not have it is enough to suggest that someone else is preventing me from enjoying my "right" to be happy.

Much of the world's mind is filled with what I call "gapism." The so-called "gap" between the rich and poor, the haves and the have-nots, is a sign, not of the natural order in which some know more and work more, but of a dire conspiracy to deprive me of what is my "right." So the mission of "rights" is to correct the world's "wrongs."

Since people have a "right" to be happy, a "divine" mission flashes in the eyes of those who would presume to make us happy by giving us our "rights." People lacking the "right" justify the takers.

So, we do not have a "right" to be happy. The assumption that we do lies behind the utopian turmoil of our times. The attempt to guarantee our "right" to be happy invariably leads to economic bankruptcy and societal coercion. By mis-understanding happiness and its gift-response condition, we impose on the political order a "mission" it cannot fulfill. We undermine that limited temporal happiness we might achieve if we are virtuous, prudent, and sensible in what we can expect in this finite world.

Chapter 25

ON THE "SHADE OF DIABOLISM"

In his Introduction to *Chaucer*, Chesterton made this striking remark about a poet: "It is primarily concerned with the fact that Chaucer was a poet. Or, in other words, that it was possible to know him without knowing anything about him." (CW XVII, 151). We may also say this same thing of the Divine Artist who fashioned this universe with His hands, in His Word. Conversely, we can know all the facts of a person's life—age, place of birth, nationality, sex, weight, height, and language spoken—and still know nothing much about this person's character. Likewise, we can know the facts of Scripture and the outlines of reason and still penetrate little into the mystery of the Godhead. We really cannot know either man or God until, freely, one or the other first invites us to know him.

The effect of the Divine Artist outside of Himself is *existence*, or, perhaps better, existing things in their order of being. Only God is His existence. Things that are not God do exist, do stand outside of nothing. We run into them all the time. In his *Autobiography*, Chesterton remarked: "Existence is still a strange thing to me; and as a stranger I give it welcome." That is a remarkably insightful sentence.

We know that we exist along with many other actual things that we name. Yet we realize that we do not "comprehend" everything about them. Something always escapes us. They just are. We did not cause them to exist. Chesterton was right to affirm that "existence" is still "strange" to him. It comes into his life as something from outside of it.

The second part of the sentence speaks of his response to existence. He does not fear it. He does not see it as a rival to himself.

He thus "welcomes" it. To "welcome" is a positive act. It does not just mean that he knows of something, or that he can describe it. The strangeness of strange things alerts us, opens our minds to what is not ourselves. We are not alone in existence

Chesterton saw Robert Louis Stevenson as someone who understood that the opposite of existence is nothing. "For these people (optimists reacting to Schopenhauer's pessimism) all the light of life was in the foreground; there was nothing in the background but an abyss. They were rather nihilists than atheists; for there is a difference between worshipping Nothing and not worshipping anything.... (Stevenson's) real distinction is that he had the sense to see that there is nothing to be done with Nothing" (CW, XVII, 75). That distinction between worshiping "Nothing" and *not* "worshiping anything" is worthy of considerable attention.

The atheist's not "worshipping anything" is rather like the Commandment not to have strange gods before us. Only now we drop God, and refuse to worship anything else. No sense of transcendence remains. There never was a time, of course, when there was simply "nothing." There was a time when only God existed, but not any other thing.

The atheist is not that far away from the First Great Commandment. He does not worship anything either. He does the opposite of what the Jews were tempted to do. Rather often, they worshiped false gods. The atheist worshiped no gods, including God. This "not worshipping anything" made the atheist the center of existence. His affirmation evaporated the world of intrinsic meaning and cause. The Nihilist worshiped "Nothing," as if it were the alternative to something.

The Nihilist and the atheist were not, however, the only players. Nothing can be juxtaposed to things that cannot be worshipped. But Scripture seems uncommonly concerned about worshipping false gods. The "fool says in his heart 'there is no God.'" But the Jews are no fools. They took to worshipping false gods. But they always pay a price. The Puritan, who also diligently read the Old Testament, and the early Protestants did not want any of the worldly trappings to interfere with their unmediated worship of God.

Chesterton took note of this mentality that sought to separate God wholly from the things He made in this way:

> And there really was implied, in varying degrees, the idea of glorifying God for his greatness rather than for his goodness. And again there occurred the natural inversion of ideas. Since the Puritans were content to cry with the Moslem: "God is great," so the descendant of the Puritans is always a little inclined to cry with the Nietzschean: "Greatness is God." In some of the really extremes, *this sentiment shaded into a sort of diabolism*" (CW, XVII, 92).

It is well to sort out the meaning in this dense passage.

Eric Voegelin found the origins of modernity among the Puritans, in a Gnosticism that made the mind of the intellectual free from dependence on *what is*. It could range freely over an empty world to concoct whatever it wanted. Luther's *sola fides* had the effect of separating philosophy and theology in such a way that they were not directed to each other.

Chesterton was remarkably perceptive to see that the exaltation of God by the Puritan and that of the Muslim were the same. Nothing in the world could point us to God. That would be to lessen Him. Indeed, the world need not be what it is. In the Muslim version, Allah could decree that good and evil were interchangeable. To limit God to the good was to limit his power. This is what is really worshipped.

So why does Chesterton bring up here the issue of shading over into "diabolism"? What is characteristic of Satan is likewise calling good evil and evil good. Nihilism is simply the worship of nothing. Good and evil do not appear in "nothing," only in existing things, indeed only in existing rational things. The atheist worships no existing thing, including God. He maintains he can explain existence without God. He can't. The Puritan and the Muslim tell us that "God is great," which is true.

But nothing in the existing world, it is said, can lead us to God, almost as if the Divine Artist was wasting His time fashioning a creation in which rational beings were found. If we press the greatness of God too far, we give Him the power to make good evil. Once we lodge this power in the Godhead, all bets are off. We can no longer distinguish good and evil in this world, in our lives and culture. We seem, in fact, to be arrived at this point. The "natural inversion of ideas" has occurred in our very midst. The "extremes" are already among us and in power. Our sentiments have "shaded over into a sort of diabolism"—not Nihilism, not atheism.

Chapter 26

ON THE FRAGILITY OF ISLAM

Islam is the longest-lasting, closed, unchanging socio-religious culture to appear among men. Its very idea is that everyone over time should worship Allah in the same way, with the same simple doctrine. The major change Islam looks to is not modernization or objective truth but, in a stable world, the submission to Allah of all men under a caliphate wherein no non-believers are found.

We still look back at communism, at least the non-oriental variety, with some astonishment in this regard. Almost no one thought it could "fall" without a major military encounter. That it disintegrated so quickly and so completely seems incomprehensible to anyone but a John Paul II. He understood its frailty, its failure to understand the human soul and its origins.

Islam is far older than Marxism. In the seventh century of our era, Islam appeared suddenly almost out of nowhere. It rapidly spread, mostly by military conquest. Its immediate victims were the Byzantine Christian lands and the Persian Empire. Both proved incapable of rising to their own defense. Islamic armies eventually conquered North Africa, the Mediterranean islands, much of Spain, the Balkans, the Near East, the vast land area from southern Russia to India and Afghanistan and even parts of China. Indonesia was a more commercial conquest.

Later efforts of Europe to regain some of these conquered lands worked for a while. The Crusades ultimately failed though they indirectly prevented further Muslim conquest of the rest of Europe. Spain, Greece, and parts of the Balkans managed to regain their lands. But the control of the Muslim lands by European powers in the 18th and 19th Centuries made little real inroads into Islam itself. Islam was exposed to western power and science, but that did not effect any significant inner conversion, except perhaps for Muslim confusion about its own lack of science and technology.

The Muslim conversion of former Christian lands seems to be permanent. What few Christians are left in these lands are second-class citizens. They are under severe pressure to convert or emigrate. Many forces within Islam desire a complete enclosure of Islam that would exclude any foreign power or religion. The Muslim world is divided into the area of peace and the area of war; the latter is what Islam does not yet control.

So with this background, why talk of the "fragility" of Islam? This instability arises from the status of the text of the Qur'an as an historical document. The Qur'an is said to have been dictated directly in Arabic by Allah. It has, as it were, no prehistory, even though it did not come into existence till a century or so after Mohammed.

Scholars, mostly German, have been working quietly for many decades to produce a critical edition of the Qur'an that takes into consideration what is the "pre-history" of the Qur'an. Due to the Muslim belief that any effort to question the Qur'an's text is blasphemy, the enterprise is fraught with personal risk to the researchers. The idea that the text cannot be investigated, of course, only feeds suspicion that even Muslims worry about its integrity.

Much of the philosophy within Islam, as we know, had roots in scholars who were originally Christian or Persian. This is well recorded in Robert Reilly's *The Closing of the Muslim Mind*. But even more, the Qur'an itself seems to be composed of many elements from Christian or Hebrew scripture. The very word Qur'an has roots in liturgical books.

The systematic denial in the Qur'an itself of the Trinity and the Incarnation, the reducing of Christ from the Messiah to another prophet forces us to inquire about the connection between the Qur'an and Judaeo-Christian Scriptures. The broader claim that Mohammed's "revelation" rewrote and made obsolete the earlier revelation needs direct confrontation.

The ecumenical movement has limited relations to Islam pretty much to areas of mutual agreement. This is well enough. But one cannot ignore the issue of truth about a text and the grounds on which it is based.

Religion or faith, even in Islam through Averroes, has been conceived as a myth designed to keep the people quiet. The scholars could quietly let the caliphs and the imams rule if the intelligentsia were left free to pursue philosophy, which was conceived to be anti-Qur'an in the sense that the Qur'an did not hold up to scrutiny about its claims.

The fragility of Islam, as I see it, lies in a sudden realization of the ambiguity of the text of the Qur'an. Is it what it claims to be? Islam is weak militarily. It is strong in social cohesion, often using severe moral and physical sanctions. But the grounding and unity of its basic document are highly suspect. Once this becomes clear, Islam may be as fragile as communism.

Chapter 27
ON THE POINT OF HUMAN EXISTENCE

My brother-in-law sent me a "Calvin and Hobbes," a cartoon series I confess not to read much in spite of its explicit metaphysical and theological overtones. The scene begins in a schoolroom. The school-marm is standing before the blackboard instructing the class on its next move: "If there are no questions, we'll move on to the next chapter." From the side, not seeing any face, we see a voice — "I have a question."

Next Calvin is at his desk, quite alert. The teacher replies: "Certainly, Calvin, what is it?" Calvin responds in good Aristotelian form: "What is the point of human existence?" The teacher comes down to his desk and explains to a dejected Calvin: "I meant any questions about the subject at hand." We see a weak "Oh" from Calvin. Finally, he is alone at his desk, looking down dismally at the assigned chapter muttering to himself: "Frankly, I'd like to have the issue resolved before I expend any more energy on this" (3-3-92).

I am not sure if my brother-in-law sent me this cartoon in order to see if I had any answer to Calvin's question. Actually, I rather like St. Ignatius' "point": "Man was created to praise, reverence, and serve God and thereby to save his soul." No school-marm is allowed to say that; few professors would dare to.

I am inclined to think, however, that people who go around constantly asking about the "point of existence" can be rather overbearing, even boorish. I have a certain sympathy for the teacher who will not be distracted by students' initial metaphysical wonderings designed mostly to distract her from the subject at hand. The young Calvins of this world are not going to "get this issue resolved" before they get on with their lessons, if only because their lessons are also included in the point of their existence. This world is filled with many beautiful things, as Augustine told us. It is not subversive to the point of our existence properly to notice them. Indeed, we probably need to notice quite a few of these beautiful things before we will even be capable of grasping the point of our existence.

Yet, Calvin is right. The "higher things" are seldom one of the "subjects at hand" in our universities. E. F. Schumacher, a young Calvin if there ever was one, recalling his education at Oxford as a young man, wrote something quite similar: "All through school and university I had been given maps of life and knowledge on which there was hardly a trace of many of the things that I most cared about and that seemed to me to be of the greatest possible importance to the conduct of my life" (*A Guide for the Perplexed*, 1).

All of this brooding is an echo of Allan Bloom's unsettling remark that the unhappiest people in our societies are those students in the twenty or thirty best universities who are brought up on, and themselves mostly accept, a diet of impossible relativism as the basis of their lives. Yes, I think that if any Catholic universities are included in this list, that the situation is not in fact markedly different.

Actually, I began to think of these things because I was reading a passage in Boswell, a passage that seems to address itself to Calvin, Schumacher, and Bloom in a way. "Dr. Johnson was very kind this evening, and said to me," a pleased Boswell recollected in 1766,

> "You have now lived five-and-twenty years, and you have employed them well." "Alas, Sir, (said I,) I fear not. Do I know history? Do I know mathematicks? Do I know the law?" <u>Johnson</u>. "Why, Sir, though you may know no science so well as to be able to teach it, and no profession so well as to be able to follow it, your general mass of knowledge of books and men renders you very capable to make yourself mastery of any science, or fit yourself for any profession."

If we reflect on this wonderful passage, we can see that it is the old idea of liberal arts that governs the thought of Johnson about young five-and-twenty Boswell.

At five-and-twenty, Boswell did not need to know history and mathematicks and law as if he were a professional. Indeed, it would be dangerous if he did. If he knew any one of these things as a professional, he would not know nearly so well all that which would enable him to learn them all, his "general mass of knowledge of books and men."

Does this mean at five-and-twenty the young Boswell knew the point of human existence, even if he was not proficient in history, mathematicks, and law?

Three years later, Boswell discussed the issue of predestination with Johnson. For Boswell this doctrine was an open and shut case of determinism. Johnson's refusal to admit this intolerable attribute of the Divinity as irreconcilable with "the full system of moral government" was due, in Boswell's mind, to Johnson's early piety, not to any fault in Boswell's analysis of this perplexing issue.

Boswell then decided further to test Johnson on the beliefs of the "Roman Catholicks" one by one. It comes as something of a shock today to recall the "reasonableness" of these too often neglected doctrines of the faith.

Boswell. "What do you think, Sir, of Purgatory...?" *Johnson.* "Why, Sir, it is a very harmless doctrine. They are of opinion that the generality of mankind are neither so obstinately wicked as to deserve everlasting punishment, nor so good as to merit being admitted to the society of blessed spirits; and therefore that God is graciously pleased to allow of a middle state, where they may be purified by certain degrees of suffering. You see, Sir, there is nothing unreasonable in that."

Boswell. "But then, Sir, their Masses for the dead?" *Johnson.* "Why, Sir, if once it is established that there are souls in purgatory, it is as proper to pray for *them*, as for our brethren of mankind who are yet in this life."

Boswell. "The idolatry of the Mass?" *Johnson.* "Sir, there is no idolatry in the Mass. They believe God is there and they adore Him."

Boswell. "The worship of saints?" *Johnson.* "Sir, they do not worship saints; they invoke them; they only ask their prayers."

Boswell. "Confession?" *Johnson.* "Why, I don't know but that it is a good thing. The Scripture says, 'Confess your faults to one another,' and the priests confess as well as the laity. Then it must be considered that their absolution is only upon repentance, and often upon penance also. You think your sins may be forgiven without penance, upon repentance alone."

What is the point of this brief catechesis from Samuel Johnson on the beliefs of Roman Catholicks? What is the point of human existence? "You see, Sir, there is nothing unreasonable in that."

Are these doctrines also the things we most need to know about and are of greatest importance in the conduct of our lives? Are our five-and-twenty year-old immortal souls confused because, unlike Johnson, they cannot reason clearly about what is actually held?

In an essay originally published in 1930, Henri de Lubac wrote, to these points, "There is no better way...for *giving an explanation* of our Faith —as we have the duty to do—than to work with all our strength for its *understanding*" (*Theological Fragments*, Ignatius, 1989, p. 98).

Linus and Snoopy are lying under a tree. The dog is looking at the small human who says, "It's too much for me to take. I can't stand it!" Linus rolls over on his stomach, hands on his chin, head of dog over his back, "It's pretty disheartening to find out your own sister wishes you'd never been born."

Linus then looks the dog directly in the face, to continue, "'Never been born'. . . . Good grief! Do you know what that means? Just stop to think about it...." Finally, standing back under the tree, Linus concludes: "Why, the theological implications alone are staggering!"

What is the point of human existence? What if someone wishes we did not ever exist? What if we did not in fact exist? No purgatory, no everlasting punishment, no saints, no predestination, no Mass, no confession, no problems?

Will our general mass of knowledge of books and men save us from such conclusions? It should help, I think. "Man is made to

praise, reverence, and to serve God, and thereby to save his soul."
Once he has this view straight, the rest follows, at least if we can
calmly understand how there is nothing unreasonable in existence,
in the truths and practices handed down to us. Human existence
does have a point. There are indeed theological implications just
in being born.

The implied teaching in Linus' reflection about his sister and
his being born is, I suspect, that if our sisters, who, like Linus' sister
Lucy, often know us so well, are glad that we were born, we can
be pretty sure that life is a grace and not the despair Linus knew it
would be if Lucy were serious.

This is, after all, the great thing about our existence, the great
thing that denies the determinism eight-and-twenty Boswell claimed
to have found in God's foreknowledge about our coming to be.
Not merely are we born on this earth, but we are given freedom to
choose whether we think what happened both to ourselves and to
all others because we were born was indeed good. Was it or was it
not pointless? How we choose to think about the ultimate worth
of our own existence, in the end, has much to do with the point of
our existence.

Chapter 28

ON AMERICAN UN-EXCEPTIONALISM

Is the United States just like other nations? Or is there something unique about its founding that resolves the central issue of politics, namely what is the best practical regime for most people? If I read the current president (Obama) correctly, he does not think that the United States has anything exceptional about it. Indeed, he apparently thinks that the very notion of this exceptionalism has caused havoc in the world. With a quasi-Marxist analysis, America has "exploited" the world to its benefit. The president's mission is to set things right by reducing America to size.

We have not explained to the world, as many think we can and should, how it is that the nations can benefit themselves by embracing certain unique American ideas of freedom, responsibility, rule of law, enterprise, and limits of government. Rather, we need to withdraw because our ideas are harmful to the poor. Not a few conservatives hold a similar thesis. The difference is that the president seems to think that the best regimes are the European socialist-welfare configurations that put most things in the control of government, while the latter think that America is unique, decentralized, but un-exportable.

In reflecting on the nature of our polity, however, we must keep in mind the classical thinkers, particularly Plato and Aristotle. If we be Christians, we recall that the New Testament says little about politics—render to Caesar, be obedient to the emperor, love thy neighbor. This relative indifference to politics is a theological compliment to reason, to what it can figure out by itself. *Pace* the liberationists of whatever stripe, revelation is not concerned with the political or economic structures of this world. We are given brains to deal with such things. Rather, it is concerned with eternal life and how it is achieved in any polity, good or bad. Granted that politics can obstruct and obscure the proper hierarchy of human goods, still revelation did not reveal what reason could figure out without it.

Christianity does presuppose that man is a certain kind of being. He is free to reject or accept what he is. In either case, acceptance or rejection, consequences follow from free human actions. In more healthy times, we would call this *natural law*. We do not call it so today. Why? Because how we choose to live requires that we reject *any* implication that an objectively right and wrong way of living exists, especially a right and wrong way that deals with sex, marriage, and the family. This conscious denial of an identifiable and normative human nature brings to our consciousness the classical descriptions of the relation between polity and ways of personal living.

In practice, we are carrying out the Greek cycle of regimes that lead from oligarchy to democracy to tyranny, all of a most genteel nature. In our concern with exceptionalism and un-exceptionalism, we failed to notice that human nature is going pretty much along the paths that were sketched out for us particularly by Aristotle and Plato. The Platonic principle that the order of polity is but a reflection of the order of soul seems to be a perfectly accurate way to conceive the real nature of our public order. Gradually, but with increasing quickness, the public order has been declining along the lines that lead from the classic definition of the end of democracy to the classic definition of the end of tyranny. These ends were always seen to be related.

The central political issue remains that of personal virtue or its lack manifested in identifiable vice, however it be named. While government may make either virtue or vice easier or more difficult through law, it cannot dictate what goes on in the souls of the citizens. The definition of oligarchy was wealth as a definition of personal happiness. Democracy placed liberty at its center. At first sight this freedom sounds noble until we realize that it is a liberty that has no definitive content as such. It is whatever we want. Government exists to provide our wants. The political form of democracy does not oppose such "liberty" but fosters it and elevates it to the status of legal "rights." In such a regime, the discipline needed for virtue disappears.

In a multi-chaos of conflicting desires arise men, probably relatively young and articulate, who can sway the people. The most eloquent associates himself with what he thinks the people should want. He sets himself against any remains of wealth or virtue that might resist him. He takes the side of the "poor." He orders the polity to himself and his own ideas which have no further grounding than what he wants.

Initially, this "leader of the people" achieves his end by promising the people what they want, by putting more and more of them under direct control of government agencies. The people themselves think that they have a "right to everything." But the new leader is not their servant but their master. His mission is the achievement of his own ideas and friends. The people, lacking their own virtue, pass from an envious benevolence to the status of subjects, not citizens.

The circle is logically complete. It goes on whether we notice it or not. In the beginning, America might have been "exceptional," but, on more careful analysis, it looks now pretty much as Aristotle and Plato described a regime that rejected virtue and the knowledge thereof. Or, as I have often said, the most difficult and dangerous task in political philosophy is accurately to describe, in terms of reason, the real character of the regime in which one lives.

Chapter 29
ON TRUTH

The Catholic Church, almost alone in the modern world, talks about truth. Truth can be both defined and understood. From the fact that no finite mind can understand everything *that is*, it does not follow that such a finite mind knows nothing. Nor is the affirmation that "truth exists and we can know it" arrogance or hubris. The denial of truth and its possibility is closer to arrogance and pride. Refusal to acknowledge that something is true partakes, in its own way, in the mystery of iniquity, in not wanting to know.

Benedict XVI spoke of the centrality of truth (*L'Osservatore Romano*, July 13, 2011). "Tradition tells us that theology is the science of faith." But "is this true?" the pope asks. Many think that faith ceases when we know. This is true in some things. But does "faith cease to be faith when it becomes a science?" Modern "science" makes this issue compelling. Modern scientific method is but one way of knowing, not the only way.

Theology has paid most attention to the notion of "scientific" history. What exactly happened? A theology based solely on history seems only concerned with the past. Faith is of the present. Faith could also be a means of "instruction" about how to live, a psychology or sociology. We still need to know whether living the way the faith indicates is "true." Lots of "beliefs" and "ways" are not.

The question remains: "Is what we believe true?" We must ask ourselves this question and answer it. This affirmation that it is true is definitely what Catholicism holds about its teachings. Benedict recalls Tertullian: Christ called Himself "Truth" not "Custom." In the ancient world, custom meant the religious rites of a pagan people, how they honored their gods. Benedict tells us that "The revolutionary aspect of Christianity in antiquity was precisely its break with 'custom' out of love for the truth." Christ is called *Logos*. This means reason. *Deus Veritas est.*

What does this affirmation mean for us? We are expected to respond to God with our own *logos*, our own reason. The divine revelation is also directed to our minds as minds. Our reason is derived from the divine reason. "Christian faith, by its very nature, must bring theology into being, must question itself on the reasonableness of faith." Faith is not imagination or fantasy, not that there is anything wrong with these as such.

Here Benedict turns to a passage from St. Bonaventure. Reason has a "double" meaning. Reason can make itself "the supreme and ultimate judge of all things." If I cannot understand something, I conclude that it is not intelligible, not that I don't get it. This approach elevates my finite reason to supremacy.

In response, the pope curiously cites a passage from Psalm 95. The people saw God's work but still "tested," that is, doubted, Him. We can see and not believe. "Experimental reason today appears as the sole form of rationality that is declared scientific. What cannot be scientifically proven or disproven falls outside the scientific sphere."

The pope previously pointed out that science investigates things composed with matter or quantity. If quantity is lacking in a being, scientific method cannot deal with it. We know things, the highest things, but they are not material. "Yet there is a limit to such a use of reason. God is not an object for human experimentation. He is the Subject and manifests himself solely in the relationship of person to person: this is part of the person's essence."

What does it mean to say that God is not an "object" but a "subject?" If God is the "subject" of theology, we can only know or reason about Him if we know what He has told us about Himself. We find this information in revelation. Once we have it, we can think about it, figure out how it can be true. If we make God a "problem" or an object to be investigated by mathematical or such methods, we will never find Him as that is not His nature or being.

We not only want to know something but love it if it is worthy. "Love desires to know better what it loves." This is a fundamental principle. Love does not "blind" us, but enables us to see what is really there in a person. The Godhead is a Trinity of persons. Love seeks a true knowledge of what the other is.

Reason directs itself to know God. If we lack reasoned love, "the great questions of humanity fall outside the context of person and are left to irrationality." Theology must know its real Subject. "The initiative for this journey is with God, who has placed in human hearts the desire to seek his Face." *Deus Veritas est. Homo est animal rationale*—God is truth. Man is a rational animal.

Chapter 30
ON GENERAL WOLFE'S PREFERENCE

Will Cuppy (1884–1948) was born in Auburn, Indiana, and he is buried there. He attended the University of Chicago and dithered with a higher degree. He wrote a number of books, the first of which I have. It is called: *How to Get from January to December*. His two most famous books are entitled: *The Decline and Fall of Practically Everybody* and *How to Tell Your Friends from the Apes*. I still laugh every time I think of that latter title. The "Decline and Fall" title is rather a reminder of the Fall and of the finiteness of all thing not God.

Collections of humorous essays are rare finds. They can be profound in their own way. We are inclined to think that such books do not reveal intelligence, only frivolity. But Chesterton was right. The opposite of funny is not "serious," but simply "not funny." No reason exists why essays cannot be both witty and profound. The very fact that we can laugh reveals, as Aristotle implied, a mind capable of seeing the relationship in things. The man who catches the point of no jokes is the man who sees no relationships in things. The essence of intelligence is to see the relation of all things, including the highest things, to one another. This "seeing" may be why there is joy in the divinity.

Each day of the year in *How to Get from January to December* is dedicated to something. Somehow our day is better when we find out what Cuppy has to say about it. Take January 2. This is my sister's birthday, though Cuppy did not note it. He does tell us that the British General James Wolfe is born on this day in 1727. Wolfe seems to be the reason Canada is more English than French, the Battle of Quebec, the Plains of Abraham, and all that.

Cuppy notes, however, that Wolfe was no big war-monger. He was a gentleman soldier who loved literature even more than battle.

As he sailed up the St. Lawrence River the night before the battle, he is reported to have "recited to his officers" the lines from Gray's *Elegy Written in a Country Churchyard*. When he finished, he said: "Gentlemen, I would rather have written that poem than take Quebec tomorrow." Does every Canadian schoolboy know these lines? Cuppy tells us that Wolfe liked even more the sadder line: "The paths of glory lead but to the grave."

But this is sober reading of an early morning. Cuppy tells us that he preferred the earlier lines in Gray, though he could not exactly remember them. They began, he recalled: "'The lowing herds tra-la-la o'er the lea,' or something of that sort." "Anyhow," Cuppy confesses with Wolfe, "It's one of my favorite poems." One is hard pressed to find a better way to spend January 2 of any year.

I find it difficult to resist anything about Doctor Samuel Johnson. His birthday, Cuppy tells us, was on September 18 in 1709, in Litchfield, Staffordshire, England. Johnson "wrote a dictionary," the first English one, in fact. Johnson in a famous remark said that a dictionary was a very interesting work, but "It didn't seem to have much of a plot." I have found this to be true myself.

But a more serious problem arises about a dictionary, as Cuppy tells us. He had a friend who said that "The trouble with the dictionary is that you have to know how a word is spelled before you can look it up to see how it is spelled."

Cuppy recognized the perceptiveness of this issue. "Sometimes I think there is a weak link in his argument, if one could only find it." I have had this problem many times myself. But, Cuppy, metaphysician that he is, concluded: "At other times I think he may have hit on a self-evident truth." This insight is rivaled only by the Declaration of Independence and the works of Thomas Aquinas. I know that "self-evident truths" are not very popular these days, as they cramp our living styles. But it is hard to escape the logic of this one.

Not only do "Paths of glory lead but to the grave" and self-evident truths may exist, but certain facts cause us to wonder. On November 25, Cuppy tells us that someone had taken the trouble to count how many eggs a female ling cod carries. The answer is

28,361,000, in round numbers. A seventeen pound turbot made this ling look amazing. Lady Turbot had 9,161,000 eggs. A lesser fish, the lowly pound and a half perch, contained 191,000.

The figures are astounding. A cod fish can have over nine million eggs and even a goldfish from two to seventy thousand. Cuppy recognized that we must take the measure of these figures. I will pass over the temptation to comment on the *Wall Street Journal's* article telling us that some college female students sell their own ova for around $10,000. The human female carries in her lifetime about five hundred. Cuppy himself would not have had to worry about this latter issues, but he still wondered about the abundance of eggs that lady fish produce.

Cuppy's final line is this: "A sunfish sometimes has 300 million eggs. What are they trying to prove?" One cannot but be amused at Cuppy's last question in the light of his statistics. We have the impression that something "self-evident" is going on here, something to do with the beginnings and ends of the paths of glory. The purpose of begetting is to keep a species of living things in existence. But, as Plato said, ultimately, in the case of human beings, in the case of minds capable of seeing relationships, the end of the love manifested in begetting is the immortality of the soul–not of the species but of every individual begotten, the further issue of "eternal life." Yes, this "What are they trying to prove?" intimates that often the humorist is the metaphysician and the theologian.

Chapter 31
On Lying

Daniel Mahoney's book, *The Other Solzhenitsyn,* follows the judicious pattern with which Mahoney, in previous books, treated de Gaulle, Aron, Manent, and other writers. We note that one of the commandments tells us not to "lie." After reading Mahoney, we suspect that the "lie," not murder, adultery, or stealing, is the most heinous of all the sins. Certainly, in Solzhenitsyn's judgment, it was the "lie" that was the foundation of modern totalitarianism. The "lie" made its killing of so many possible. Its lie embraced almost anyone who went along with it either out of agreement or fear. The great courage of Solzhenitsyn was revealed not so much in suffering the concentration camp as in his adamant refusal to lie about the totalitarian order in which he lived. Not to lie means to tell the truth about *what is.*

The story of George Washington never telling a lie perhaps witnessed to something more fundamental in our politics and culture than we are wont to admit. To function at all, any justice system must require witnesses publically to profess that they answer questions truthfully. To "perjure" oneself means precisely to tell a lie when one has sworn that he is telling the truth. For a republic to be founded on the principle of "no official lies" is surely a good thing. We know that many men lie for many reasons. We deal with this fact under the headings of justice, repentance, and, if appropriate, clemency. We do not justify lying on the grounds that many in practice lie and know they lie.

The "lie" is made famous in political philosophy both by Machiavelli and Plato. For Machiavelli, the lie was a tool in the arsenal of the politician, to be used, like truth, if it was deemed helpful to stay in power. But Machiavelli's politician knew that he was lying. He was not claiming it was "true."

Plato's "noble lie," however, was not really a lie. It relates to what Solzhenitsyn had in mind. To those who live in untruth, the truth will seem like or be called a "lie." Modern ideology is a description of the world that does not correspond to reality. It seeks to implant, either by force or persuasion, an untrue system on human reality. This is why, as Solzhenitsyn said, ideology must live by the "lie" and by force, why it must punish truth tellers who identify what is real, who affirm that a Gulag is a systematic killing of actual human beings for no reason but to maintain the ideology in power.

Plato is often blamed for founding such ideology. But he is really the greatest of the opponents to ideology. The best city is in "mind" or "speech'. Actual cities can never be perfect. To seek to make cities in this world perfect is the very essence of ideology. Man's final end is transcendent to actual cities. To accomplish this imposition in this world, it is always necessary to use lies and force, as Solzhenitsyn never tired of showing.

What is a "lie"? A lie is a statement, presented as fact, that does not conform to a reality that we did not make or legislate into existence. Recently, the director of the State of California Health Department, in imposing, i.e., forcing abortion provisions on Catholic universities, stated: "Abortion is a basic health care service," (Catholic League, August 22, 2014). This is a public lie. Abortion is the direct killing of a human life. It is always lethal to the child and mostly deleterious to the mother and father. It is also a moral delict on the part of those who perform it and those who legally make it possible. To choose to live by and enforce this lie is to embrace ideology. This is the most hateful of all kinds of lies. It is a lie responsible for killing more actual human beings than all the Gulags of the world ever thought of—over one billion three hundred million abortions in the world since 1980.

What does a lie do? It makes communication between human beings impossible. To state that killing a child is "health care" is incoherent. The essence of a lie substitutes something plausible for what is true. The birth of a child and the health of a mother are goods. But motherhood, fatherhood, and childhood are not in opposition to each other, but part of the same coordinate reality. To separate them is to lie about them.

The broader issue of lying needs stating. If what I affirm is a lie, I cut myself off from reality. If I insist on making my lies public, even public law, I must not permit the truths that my lies deny to appear in public. I must prevent their statement. This is why lies and force are twins. The opposite of the lie is truth. This is the real issue that Solzhenitsyn spent his life affirming.

Chapter 32

ON THE "END TIME"

A friend wrote in early December that this is the "end of the liturgical year." In the readings of Mass and the Breviary, we are given selections from Daniel, Joel, Matthew, and others that call attention to the truth that time, as we know it, will end, and, it seems, not always very pleasantly for everyone. We are told that time will end at a moment when we least expect it. Women will be working in the fields. There will be marriage and giving in marriage, weeping and gnashing of teeth. Need we pay any attention to these bizarre accounts? Few if any of us expect this end to fall on Advent or on New Year's Eve. In the book of Joel, the final event is scheduled to happen in the Valley of Jehoshaphat (sometimes identified with the Valley of the Kedron, near Jerusalem).

This "end time" is pictured not merely as an end, but as a judgment, a word we do not like even though, if we lacked the capacity to judge, we would cease to be human beings endowed with reason and will. It pays to be careful about what we do not like. The phrase "judge not lest you be judged," was not designed to reduce us to complete silence or to idiocy. Further, we know not the day nor the hour, but we should be prepared. Our lives are "purposeful." They are not given to us just so that we can pass the time of day waiting for something to happen, though sometimes even that is all right.

How is it possible that an account can be made of the being and actions of our lives? This "all-knowing" postulates a divine intelligence. A major purpose in denying any deeper consideration of this issue is to avoid facing the suspicion that we are not completely alone. Yet, the first, or divine, "intelligence" is not "part" of the universe, but transcends it. What we are and do in this world, however, makes a difference. Our deeds and thoughts are both known and remembered. We are tiny, passing beings, but not totally insignificant beings, none of us. Our significance includes lives that deliberately reject what is right and good. Evil in the universe is not the result of some horrid divine plot. It results from the willing rejection of a glorious estimation and elevation of the kind of being we are.

At first sight, this approach might seem preposterous. Yet, even science and science fiction are full of speculations about making contact with the voices and deeds of past earthly and cosmic dwellers if our instruments are delicate enough or are sent in the right direction. Men are reluctant to accept their loneliness and finiteness in the universe. Is such reluctance silly? I suspect not.

Is it possible that an order or plan makes sense of this expectation of the "end time"? If there is such a "plan," where would we find it? It is at this point that Christian thinking about what its scriptures say on the subject comes into play. In the "beginning," as I like to say, God did not create from nothing a cosmic order, then, seeing it sitting out there, wonder what He would do with it.

It is the other way around. What God was initially interested in was not the cosmos. The cosmos as cosmos knows nothing. It may be a product of God's creative intelligence, but it cannot, as it were, "do" what God is. Christian revelation has two basic things to tell us about God, both of these things relate to wonderments of the philosophers pursuing reason as far as it could go.

The first thing we are told is that God is not monolithic. Otherness exists in God. So God does not need the universe to give Him something He lacks. How is this otherness described to us? As a relation of Persons in the being they are. It is best described as love. God "needs" nothing further than Himself. Thus, as Plato said, we are the "playthings" of God. This wording is not flippant. It indicates a delight about our being. It is a word that takes us to the essential relationship we have with God, namely that He created us because He first loved us, not because He needed us.

But if this understanding is true, the second part of Christian revelation, the redemption, comes into play. God had to give us an opportunity freely to know and love Him. That is what goes on in this world. It grounds what happens in the cosmos. The "end times" close God's purpose. This is why there must be judgment. What did we do in our time, whenever it was? Redemption was God's response to our not loving Him in the first place. It is God's final effort to enable us freely to see and love the truth, the *Logos*. This is why it says: "And after this, the Judgment." This final judgment is the divine acceptance of our freedom; however we chose to live it.

Chapter 33

ON THE CITY OF GOD

With a class, I read Augustine's *City of God*. Augustine took about thirteen years to write it; it took us nineteen class days, reading 57 pages a clip. Anyone claiming to have read all the works of Augustine, a famous quip goes, "is a liar." The same might be said of anyone, including Schall and his students, who says that he understands every aspect of the *City of God*. In English, the book is 1091 Penguin edition pages. It requires attention.

At the semester's beginning, I told a class of about seventy students that, at least once in our lives (it is not enough, I know), we should read this remarkable book that bears the Christian title (*De Civitate Dei*) of Plato's *Republic*. The students were to look on its reading as an adventure, as great as any that they will ever undertake. But it is also a task. I asked them if they were willing to try it. I did not want to read only "parts," the bane of academic life. Under Schall's cold gaze, they agreed. I think, not reluctantly. With some awe, they mostly enjoyed it. Its reading is one of life's soul-moving experiences, like reading the *Metaphysics* of Aristotle, or the *Brothers Karamazov*, or the Epistle to the Romans.

Throughout the book, Augustine keeps explaining to the reader the order of the book. Augustine knows it is a difficult read, whose parts need constant repetition. At the end of book 10, Augustine explains: "The first five books (of twenty-two books) have been written against those who imagine that the gods are to be worshipped for the sake of the good things of this life, the latter five against those who think that the cult of the (Roman) gods should be kept with a view to the future life after death."

When Augustine finishes with these dubious theses about the pagan gods, not much is left of them. The next twelve books, in three groups of four books each, are devoted to the two cities, the City of God and the City of Man. "I shall treat of their origin, their development and their destined ends."

The occasion for writing this remarkable book was a letter Augustine received from his friend Marcellus. He wanted some guidance on dealing with elite pagans. They witnessed the sack of Rome in 411. They concluded that the angry gods allowed this devastation of the Eternal City because its religion changed to Christianity under Constantine in 325 A.D.

Not unlike Plato's brothers in the *Republic,* who, when they wanted to hear justice praised for its own sake, turned to Socrates, the one man who might be able to deal with the question, so Marcellus turned to Augustine. Augustine knew enough classical and Roman history to point out that these pagan gods did not always protect Rome. He also knew enough philosophy to see the incoherence of the salvific claim of the pagan gods.

The *City of God* brings up for our consideration the rise and fall of nations, of whether a "purpose" is found in secular things. Earlier Christians wanted to see secular history as providential. Augustine was quite careful here. He had, as it were, bigger fish to fry. Scripture did contain factual historical events. The *City of God* is full of Augustine's examination of times and places. He knows about Caesar Augustus and Christ's birth, the time of the Crucifixion. He is himself a Roman citizen, from one of the African conquests.

But the *City of God* is not about the rise and fall of nations except in so far as they provide the arena in which what really happens in history is carried out. Augustine has two sources of knowledge, his reason and Scripture. He places them together in a coherent whole. Both arise from the same origin. Perhaps the most famous book of the *City of God* is book 19. Here he gives the 288 different philosophic definitions of happiness.

In the first chapter of book 19, we find Schall's favorite sentence in Augustine: "*Nulla est homini causa philosophandi nisi ut beatus sit—*Man has no cause to philosophize other than that he be happy."

The *City of God*, briefly, relativizes all political institutions insofar as they claim to make man eternally happy, as so many do. The City of God is composed of all of those who, in the course of their lives, in whatever place or era, choose God as their end in the plan that God reveals. The City of Man is composed of all those who, in their lives and thought, reject this gift. The purpose of the cosmos and our place within it is to make possible, in each particular case, that this decision be freely made.

Modern politics, science, and culture almost never mention that truth, which is why Christians have to return again and again to the thousand-plus pages of *The City of God*.

Chapter 34

ON WORDS FROM WODEHOUSE

I finished *Weekend Wodehouse*, a 1951 collection published in London by Herbert Jenkins. The Introduction is by Belloc. As far as I can tell neither Belloc's nor Wodehouse's England still exists. The only way to preserve what you see, Belloc wrote, is to write about it. Then it can live forever, even in this world, as long as the word and "this world" last.

Belloc writes: "For the English people, more than any other, have created in their literature living men and women rather than types and Mr. Wodehouse has created Jeeves. He has created others, but in his creation of Jeeves he has done something which may respectfully be compared to the work of the Almighty in Michelangelo's painting. He has formed a man filled with the breath of life."

Yes, that is it. Jeeves, Bertie Wooster, Pongo Twistleton, Lady Constance Keeble, the Hon. Galahad Threepwood, Adeline Smethurst, Freddie Widgeon, Mavis Peasemarch, and so many others do possess the breath of life. Chesterton said that Dickens had the same power.

In my early years, after discovering him—a notable event in the life of any man—I used to say that Wodehouse is to be read with a dictionary. But on finishing *Weekend Wodehouse*, I think I was wrong. Wodehouse does stretch one's vocabulary. But it is not the meaning of the words that is novel or unknown. It is their placement.

For instance, I did not count the number of times the word "looney" came up. It is a marvelous word. It appears in the first story—"even with an uncle within a short jump of the looney bin... ." Looney uncles, looney friends populate Wodehouse stories. The word comes either from a wobbly bird or from the moon, a kind of pleasant madness. No one would want to live in a world in which no looney characters were encountered.

The first story in *Weekend Wodehouse* begins in the Drones Club. What a perfect name for an English gentleman's club—both in its noun and its verb forms! My *Webster's Dictionary* thus defines a drone: 1) "The male of a bee that has no sting and gathers no honey, 2) One that lives on the labors of others." The verb means: "To make a sustained deep murmuring, humming, or buzzing sound." Such are not unknown features of gentlemen's clubs. The members of the Drones Club, looney or otherwise, are identified by what they usually order—Crumpets, Eggs and Beans, Small Bass.

The first scene in "Uncle Fred Flits By" concerns a "young blood" named Pongo Twistleton. His "animal spirits" cause a disturbance in the Club while the "Crumpet" was enjoying his after lunch coffee. The residents looked at the door. A "young blood," who later turns out to be a "clam," appeared in "form-fitting tweeds."

"The aspect of this young man was haggard. His eyes glared wildly and he sucked at an empty cigarette-holder. If he had a mind, there was something on it." What an amusing line! "If he had a mind, there was something on it." We are deftly left in doubt about the existence of Pongo's mind.

What struck me on again reading Wodehouse was the central place smoking played in the everyday affairs of English gentlemen. If they still smoked cigars and cigarettes at the pace they did in Wodehouse, it would be enough to replant all of Virginia in tobacco. Tobacco is now a weed to be avoided at the cost of our lives. I do not recall one line in Wodehouse that ever hinted that smoking was anything but an innocent pleasure. We seem to have the resultant health but not the innocent pleasures. Our vices are redefined, but never innocent.

A wealthy man by the name of Stoker, apparently to make amends for misjudging him, invited Bertram Wooster to dine on his yacht. Stoker probably regarded Wooster as a "bit looney." Bertie discusses with Jeeves what is the exact word to describe what

Stoker was trying to do. Jeeves suggests the French phrase *"amende honorable."* But Bertie prefers to say that Stoker offered "an olive branch."

Jeeves regards "olive branch" as acceptable, but not precise. Jeeves considered the French expression as more exact. It carries with it "the implication of remorse, or the desire to make restitution." This is what I mean by the title "Words from Wodehouse." We find in Wodehouse an exactness of language that delights us.

In an earlier story in the Blanding Castle series, Lord Emsworth described the awfulness of his having to attend an annual school function that his sister, Lady Constance, organized at his Castle. This is how Wodehouse described the situation: "A function like the Blandings Parva School Treat blurred the conception of man as Nature's Final Word." Has our human lot ever been better described?

Chapter 35

ON LINGARD'S ACCOUNT OF THE EXECUTION
OF MARY, QUEEN OF SCOTS

The 21st Century opened with Europe's specific view that its Christian heritage was not appropriate for itself. The possibility grows, either through population growth or conquest, of an expanded Islamic presence in Europe. English Catholics once looked back on the historical accounts of the Reformation and the earlier Catholic history of England. Some even read the eight volume *History of England* by the English priest, John Lingard (1771–1851). "My object is truth...," Lingard wrote, "through the work I made it a rule to tell the truth, whether it made for us or against us." Lessons can still be learned both from the forced change of a religion and from the often skewered accounts of it.

The World's Great Catholic Literature, edited by George Schuster, contains a poignant passage from Lingard on the execution of Mary, Queen of Scots. The passage reminded me of Edmund Burke's moving and critical account, in his *Reflections on the Revolution in France*, of the execution of Marie Antoinette. It also recalled Lord Acton's account of the execution by firing-squad, on June 19, 1867, of Maximilian, Emperor of Mexico. All three descriptions are of the ambiguous, largely unjust executions of elevated, noble persons, who die both with dignity and piety.

Mary was beheaded at 8 a.m. on February 8, 1587, inside Fortheringhay Castle, north of London. She was accused of plotting to kill her half-sister, Elizabeth, to whom she fled for protection from Scot enemies. According to Lingard, Mary was brought forward from her cell by the sheriff, accompanied by the Earls of Shrewsbury and Kent. She "wore the richest of her dresses, that was appropriate to the rank of a queen dowager." Her gown was red, perhaps intended as the sign of martyrdom. She remained cheerful of aspect. "She bore without shrinking the gaze of the spectators, the sight of the scaffold, the block, and the executioner; and advanced into the hall with that grace and majesty which she had so often displayed in her happier days." She intended to die as a queen and a Catholic.

As Mary mounted the scaffold, a man by the name of Pawlett offered his arm in help. Mary replied: "I thank you, Sir; it is the last trouble I shall give you, and the most acceptable service you have ever rendered me." This was Sir Amias Pawlett, whom Elizabeth had appointed as "Keeper of Mary, Queen of Scots." None of Pawlett's other "services" to Mary had been at all appreciated by her. He would have had to have been very insensitive to have missed her irony.

The executioner was from the Tower, clad in black. He was rather inept. He had to strike her three times to finish his bloody job. The lithograph print of this execution shows perhaps seventy or eighty persons present. They formally surround the block of execution. The warrant was read. Mary replied, in Lingard's words: "She would have them recollect that she was a sovereign princess, not subject to the Parliament of England, but brought there to suffer by injustice and violence. She, however, thanked her God that he had given her this opportunity of publicly professing her religion, and of declaring, as she had often before, that she had never imagined, nor compassed, nor consented to the death of the English queen, nor ever sought the least harm to her person." All her listeners were politically committed to maintain, in public at least, that this protestation was not true.

At this point, Mary was interrupted by Dr. Fletcher, Dean of Peterborough. He, Chaplain of the English Church, was to encourage her to repent. He told Mary that Elizabeth was "compelled to execute justice on her body" but that Elizabeth was "careful of the welfare of her soul." Hence, the Dean was there to "bring her (Mary) into the true fold of Christ." She was to repent of her wickedness, admit the justice of the accusation.

Mary tried to shut this unwelcome cleric up, or as Lingard gently put it, she "desired him not to trouble himself and her." Mary turned the other direction but the persistent Dean followed her with his exhortation. "To put an end to this extraordinary scene," the Earl of Shrewsbury told the Dean "to pray." The Dean, now in prayer mode, urged the same things that he had uttered in his unpleasant and unwelcome sermon.

Mary had her own devotions to attend to. She repeated in Latin some of the Psalms. She prayed in English "for Christ's afflicted Church, for her son James, and for Queen Elizabeth." Mary was in the long tradition of forgiving enemies. She also understood that she needed to attend to herself. She exclaimed: "As thy arms, O God, were stretched out upon the Cross, so receive me into the arms of thy mercy, and forgive me my sins."

Naturally, her executioners and those politically responsible for it could not let this pass without comment. The Earl of Kent replied: "Madam, you had better leave such popish trumperies, and bear him in your heart." There is a good deal of reformation theology in that remark. The Cross and the forgiveness of sins were a bit of "popish trumpery." All she needed was "in her heart," not public repentance.

Mary was equal to this sophistry: "I cannot at the same time hold in my hand the representation of his suffering, but I must at the same time bear him in my heart." Icons, statues, Crucifixes do not interfere with private or inner devotion, quite the opposite.

Mary's weeping maid-servants sought to remove her elegant robe. The executioners, "fearing to lose their usual perquisites," interfered. I take this passage to mean that, not unlike the soldiers who executed Christ, the soldiers got Mary's red robe after the execution as booty, so they did not want the maids to take it in front of their very eyes.

Evidently, the executioners themselves began to disrobe her. "The queen remonstrated, but instantly submitted to their rudeness, observing to the earls with a smile, that she was not accustomed to employ such grooms, or to undress in the presence of so numerous a company." Like Thomas More, Mary remained witty to the end. Her servants began to weep, but she put her finger to her lips indicating silence. In his last hour, Socrates had also chided his companions not to weep as they should have been prepared for death, however it comes, even by execution.

Mary then placed herself in the executioner's designated chair. A handkerchief, "edged in gold," was placed over her eyes by a man "by the name of Kennedy." On being led to the block, she knelt down and repeated in Latin: "Into thy hands, O Lord, I commend my spirit."

The sobs of the crowd disconcerted the executioner. He missed on the blows. Finally, he held up her severed head, now unrecognizable. The executioner shouted: "God save our Queen, Elizabeth." The Dean added: "So perish her (Elizabeth's) enemies." The Earl of Kent, "in a still louder voice," added, "so perisheth all the enemies of the Gospel."

Lingard designated the good Earl as simply "fanatical." These are Lingard's last words: "Not a voice was heard to cry Amen. Party feeling was absorbed in admiration and pity." By hearing no voice saying "Amen" to the exclamations of the executioner, the Dean, or the Earl, I take it that Lingard meant to indicate that no one agreed with the fanatical Earl of Kent. The witnesses to the execution of Mary, Queen of Scots, could not but admire and pity this woman who commended her spirit into the hands of the Lord before their very eyes while using the very same words that Christ himself used at His execution.

Chapter 36
ON BOTH A FATHER AND A MOTHER

We hear much loose talk of "rights." Hobbes would be pleased to see what happened to his word, one he lifted perhaps from medieval charters. The word "right" can today be used to overturn almost any thing we thought was good and holy. The term can justify almost anything we might have once thought to be aberrant. Catholic thought has doggedly sought to save the word, even when it has an equivocal meaning in the public forum, even when it means something entirely different from what such thought held it to mean.

The word "right" comes to mean what the state legislates and enforces, whatever it is. As Locke put it: "Political power, then, I take to be a right of making laws with penalties of death...." The state, we suddenly notice, is quite eager to legislate and enforce all sorts of "rights," never before heard in the land. What is new is that we are not really allowed to criticize these newly coined "rights." The First Amendment is on shaky grounds before these ruthless innovations. We no longer "hold" truths, but "rights"— and these latter rights are never "self-evident."

In *Josef Pieper—an Anthology*, we read: "A mother's love for her children is 'unconditional' in a unique fashion; that is, it is not linked with any preconditions. Because of that it corresponds to the deepest longings of children, and indeed of every human being. Maternal love doesn't have to be 'earned': and there is nothing anyone can do to lose it." Without experiencing this maternal love, we will not really understand divine or human love. We do not know what love is except by being first loved. That is the way it is.

What about a father's love? "A father...tends to set conditions; his love has to be earned. But that likewise repeats a fundamental element peculiar to all love: the desire that the beloved not only 'feel good' but that things may in truth go well for him. A mature person's love must...contain both elements, the maternal and the paternal, something unconditioned and something demanding" (43).

We have much to ponder here. If we begin not with the parents but with the child, it looks like it must have for its well-being, from its beginning in conception and birth, both kinds of love, each from its own source. Men can learn something of maternal love by living with mothers, sisters, wives and daughters. Women learn something of paternal love by being its object. The fact is that both kinds of love are "due" to any child.

Maternal and paternal loves are both human, both radically different, both needed for the whole of love. They are complementary not antagonistic to each other, not interchangeable. Not either/or but both together are required. Both are "due" in justice and in love itself to any human child. No man or woman has any independent "right" that overcomes this primary responsibility to their children.

Life, of course, finds mothers or fathers who die, leaving children without one or other parent—sometimes with neither. But if we are thinking that what "ought" to be, it is quite clear that both are to be present, to be coordinated by a common parental love and discipline that looks to the child's good. We would say that this situation is the "natural law" of our being. It looks to the good of the child. Parental love is sacrificial in this sense. It looks not to the parents' good but to the child's. This "good" is, to be sure, also the good of the parents. It allows the father to be the father and the mother to be the mother, without confusion. This latter "without confusion" is what the child needs for his own good if he is to know what it is to be a human being.

Chapter 37
ON THE WORD "VIOLENCE"

L'Osservatore Romano (30 March 2011) had these headlines: "Let the Weapons Be Silenced in Libya and Let Dialogue Begin." The implication was that "dialogue" can always take the place of arms. The *status quo* is better than change. The assumption is that the recourse to arms is not calculated or rational in its own way. Human experience often tells us that before any meaningful discussion takes place arms or violence has to be met with arms or violence. It is an odd reading of human nature and history to imply that all we have to do is lay down arms and "dialogue." Then, all will be well. Enemies, however, exist for whom "dialogue" is not a significant category except as an aid to gain their ends without arms.

In a Good Friday interview on Italian Television, Benedict XVI responded to the question of a Muslim woman: "Violence never comes from God, never helps bring anything good, but is a destructive means and not the path to escape difficulties. He (Christ) is thus a strong voice against every type of violence" (*ORE*, April 27, 2011). The papal offices are filled with pleas for peacemakers and non-violence, for dialogues of every sort.

Until recently with the killing of Christians in the Middle East, rarely do we hear discussed the issue of just war or legitimate, indeed obligatory, defense measures for ourselves or others. Popes speak regularly to Italian and Vatican police, to military chaplains, and, of course, to diplomats. In his Regensburg Address, Benedict did indicate that arenas of discussion and dialogue would have to be protected from violence for them to function. This almost unequivocal condemnation of "violence," however, seems curious to me. It lacks precision. A reasonable case can be made for the need and use of arms that is not simply "violence" in the pejorative sense.

In thinking about much of this recent turn in ecclesiastical discourse that often sounds like pacifism, I recalled the discussion of Yves Simon. He carefully distinguished between violence and coercion. In his famous *Philosophy of Democratic Government*, Simon pointed out that the term "violence" is not always simply negative. Just and unjust uses of violence are to be distinguished. "'Violence,' Simon writes, 'is sometimes used as a synonym of 'coercion.' In this sense the arrest of a burglar by a police officer is an act of violence. Anybody can see that this is loose language, to be prohibited whenever scientific rigor is needed. Not the policeman, but the burglar, is violent."

The defending one's self, whether as an individual or a nation, from unjust attacks is not itself wrong or unjust. Indeed, not to defend one's self or others may be unjust. For a nation or a city not to have enough coercive force to protect its citizens from attacks is simply irresponsible. However, as Simon said, such defense can be called "violent." "Shooting in legitimate defense is a just and violent means of protecting one's life. A war, no matter how just, is an act of violence, and so is a strike."

Violence and coercion are thus distinguished. Coercion is the use of adequate force according to man-made law, as an application of natural law. Police officers and soldiers are established to bring criminals to justice, to prevent "violence" that is not rooted in justice. This fact does not deny that occasions can occur when private citizens in lieu of the immediate aid of law have to defend themselves against criminals. Much of the "violence" of the present drug "trade" falls into this area. Nor does it mean that the police or military may not act contrary to their own law. But it does mean that the sanctioned use of force should not be called "violence" as if it has no responsible reason or cause.

The underestimation of the ruthlessness of modern criminals or ideologues is a perennial temptation of the religious mind. We see today that many fellow Christians are being killed or persecuted because the local constabulary refuses or is unable to protect them.

We also see that many men think that the use of such violence to kill infidels is legitimized by their religion. We are left sputtering to ourselves. We speak of religious freedom to those whose definition of religious freedom is that everyone should be Muslims. We appeal to a standard that is not recognized except, as we like to say, by universal law.

We are often left to accept such killings. They happen far away. We acknowledge that we cannot or will not do anything to prevent them. In any case, we need a more precise way to distinguish between efforts to prevent unjust violence and the violence itself. They do not fall within the same moral genus. To speak as though they do, it strikes me, leads to a political helplessness that makes the matters worse.

Chapter 38
ON LOVING EVERYBODY AND NOBODY

Joseph Wood asked me why I so highly esteem Samuel Johnson. Basically, I think that, if someone reads him, he has little other choice. In watching Pope Francis greet people, an issue comes up that Johnson addressed. The Pope, along with many politicians, spends much time engaging people, touching them, making them feel known to him. Pope Wojtyla was a genius at this. To the despair of police and those directing him to his next engagement, the Pope insists on chatting with almost anyone and everyone.

We are urged to love our neighbor as our selves. But the minute we try to do this, we run up against the Aristotelian caution that "He who is a friend of everybody is a friend of nobody." It is for this reason, among others, that we suspect that popes and politicians are rather lonely people. They have too many people about them. We increasingly hear it said of the president, greeter that he is on every stage, that "he seems to have no friends." Kings are said to have no friends but other kings.

This same issue came up in Boswell's recording (April 15, 1778) of Johnson's conversation with "the ingenious Quaker lady," Mrs. Knowles, with whom Johnson seems to have been a bit smitten. Evidently, Mr. Soame Jenyns had written a book, *Views of the Internal Evidence of the Christian Religion,* in which he remarked that "friendship is not a Christian virtue." Mrs. Knowles vigorously objected to this view.

But Johnson agreed with Jenyns: "Why, Madam, strictly speaking, he is right. All friendship is preferring the interest of a friend, to the neglect of, or, perhaps, against the interest of others.... Now, Christianity recommends universal benevolence, to consider all men as our brothers, which is contrary to the virtue of friendship."

Johnson next recalls the classic name given to the Quakers: "Surely, Madam, your sect must approve of this; for you call all men 'friends.'"

Mrs. Knowles responds to Johnson: We are "commanded" to call all men our friends, especially those of the "household of the faith." Johnson replies that this "household" is "very large"—meaning that such friendships must be quite diffused. To this, Mrs. Knowles observes that Christ had twelve apostles but He loved one the best. Johnson answers, "with eyes sparkling benignantly, very well, indeed, Madam. You have said very well."

This passage always reminds me of the curious impact of Christian revelation on human relationships. Aristotle knew the differing kinds of friendship—of utility, of pleasure, and those based on the highest kind of virtue. We would be fortunate if, during our lifetime, we had one or two good friends. We know that it takes a whole lifetime just to know some one person well. Does Christianity deny this? As Mrs. Knowles implied, Christianity wants it both ways, to love everyone as friends and to keep the intimacy of a few friends. This fact means that we must keep things straight.

Is there any sense in thinking that we can be friends with everyone or even of those of the "household of the faith?" Many of the problems such considerations bring up were already in Plato. In the *Republic*, he wanted to destroy the family because its inner relationships were exclusive. They tended to separate everyone into small groups. Yet, the separation of friends into a small group is the very essence of the highest forms of friendship in which we live together in life and conversation. Plato too wanted everyone to be friends. This is precisely where Aristotle stepped in to warn of the dangers of thinking everyone could be our friends in this world. Plato and Christianity had the same end: that we all be friends.

We are told that in Paradise, neither marrying nor giving in marriage, the most obvious example of exclusive and permanent friendship, occurs. Does this teaching mean that no marital friendships are found in heaven? It means that no further begetting takes place once the full number of elect is completed. But were Johnson's initial remarks right about Christianity? Does it absolve the bonds of friendship? Is this desire that we see in the popes to greet and know everyone, to urge us to be friends with everyone, an illusion?

Christianity teaches that anyone can be our friend, not just those of our city or household. Then there is the little issue of loving our enemies and those who hate us. But we are not to be naïve. Christianity does not overturn Aristotle. What it does tell us is to find what is loveable in everyone, to recognize that we are all loved by God. All our lives are but introductions, glimpses of that eternal life in which we, finally, have the abiding presence to know and love those who respond to God's call of everyone to Himself.

Chapter 39
ON THE "JEALOUS" GOD

From my youth, I can recall a haunting tango called "Jealousy."
Harry James did a version of it. Many classical artists have full or-
chestral performances. Something sultry, haunting always hovered
about this music, especially when danced by an Argentine couple.
Jealousy (from *zelosus*) was a vice that hovered about something
sacred. It was not just envy, itself a most spiritual vice. The love of
a man and woman was not to be broken, even by themselves. Fi-
delity and jealousy are related.

The Breviary during the Third Week of Lent reads from Exo-
dus. Here, Yahweh tells Moses that He has driven out the "Amor-
ites, Canaanite, Hittites, Perizzites, Hivites, and Jebusites."
Whenever I see that passage, I think of Walker Percy's question:
"Why are there no Hittites in New York City?" At last count,
though we have just about everything else, we find no Perizzites or
Hivites either. But it is the same unspoken theological point.

In this passage, the Hebrews are warned about the worship of
false gods. No covenants are to be made with such folks with their
alien gods. "Tear down their altars; smash their sacred pillars, and
cut down their sacred poles." This severe action probably could
not be carried out today as these monuments would be protected
by some historical trust ordinance. Little imagination, however, is
needed to see why the Lord was annoyed by them.

Next the Lord says to Moses: "You shall not worship any other
god, for the Lord is 'the Jealous One.' A jealous God is He."

In his *Shakespeare's Politics,* writing on *Othello,* Allan Bloom
provocatively remarked that the jealousy portrayed in the plots of
Shakespeare could never have happened in Greek drama. Why? For
the Greeks, the suspicion of marital infidelity was treated as a

comedy. In Shakespeare, however, even its suspicion, provoked by Iago's machinations, leads to death.

Bloom remarks that love is a needy thing, a view that may be Jewish, but is not Christian in sentiment. Bloom invokes the notion of the Jealous God as the cause of a difference between the love in Christian times and that of the Greeks. The issue is Yahweh's exclusiveness. Yahweh was like a young husband who expects his bride's love to be directed only to him and vice versa. What is new in the universe is that this marital love falls within the love found in the Trinity. It is not a needy love, but a complete love.

Certainly, the Old Testament reveals a purification of the idea of the gods in the light of the One God whom alone we shall worship. Indeed, one might say the same of Socrates and Plato who are both shocked with the foibles and sins of the many gods of Olympus. Socrates and Plato look to the Good. Both Yahweh and the Good are, in a way, "hidden" gods. Moses longs to see the face of Yahweh; Plato cannot stand what keeps changing.

But the "jealousy" of God teaches us much. Some loves are exclusive by nature. This is why they can come under the law. Other loves cannot be exclusive in the same way. C. S. Lewis and Benedict, in *Deus Caritas Est*, make the same distinctions between *Eros, Agape,* and *Philia.* Lewis adds *storge,* the affection we have for animals. The only human institution in which the three forms of love are united is in the marriage of a man and a woman.

Benedict calls *Agape* the love that comes down from Him who is love. It is creative and freely given. *Philia* refers to the differing kinds of friendship. It is the being together in great and little causes, side by side. *Eros* is the love that results in babies. But *Eros* does not know that or even intend it other than knowing generally that this one activity is the only one in which love is productive in babies. What is loved is already a gift.

To confuse these loves is at the root of most tragedy in our confused time. To want *Eros* without babies, on the grounds that the couple can absorb each other, leads not to life but to death. This latter is what *Tristan und Isolda* and the tale of Aristophanes in the *Symposium* were about.

The point of the "jealous" God was that He alone was worthy of complete love, since He was its source. The point of the exclusiveness of marriage is that its love is only valid when it is open to babies, when it recognizes that each partner has origin not in him or herself but in the divine exemplar in which each was called to be. What is begotten of this love is a life itself open to the same one love, the Trinitarian love found within the Godhead.

Chapter 40
ON OLD BOOKS AND OLD PROFESSORS

For an academic who has spent his life urging, insisting, and demanding that students keep good books that they have read and marked, that they not sell them, and that they have their own libraries, I have suddenly experienced a soul-moving shock. Books, like Schall himself, grow old. They are heavy and difficult to transport. Any librarian or book seller, I know, could affirm these things. But somehow, with my own books, they did not age or have weight. The fact is that books, as such, do not age or have weight. What ages and weighs are the paper on which they are written, the binding, and the covers. For a book is only accidentally a physical thing. But analogous to our bodies, it needs something to bear its reality, its soul, something to make it visible.

When Joseph Ratzinger was elected pope, he meticulously moved his substantial personal library into papal quarters so it would retain its order. Presumably something similar will happen as he moves to his new apartments. And yet, the books of a library sometimes do and sometimes do not outlast their owners' lives. In my later classes, my copy of Cicero's *Selected Letters*, with its famous essay "On Old Age," was rapidly falling apart, as was my copy of Nietzsche's *Beyond Good and Evil*. While I had a second copy of the former, I did not bother to purchase another copy of the latter. I just was careful not to let it fall apart before the eyes of my class.

As a physical object, a book is the product of a craft. It can hold doors open. A book, no matter what its content, can be a handsome object, something we like to hold, look at, and show off, if it is noteworthy. My 1931 two-volumes-in-one edition of Boswell's *Life of Johnson* was falling apart when I packed it to be trucked to California. But I did not want to part with it. It had notes in it, markings, a glowing antiquity, not that 1931 is ancient. My sister was born in that year. Paper books, which were never intended to last too long, do fall apart more easily after a few decades.

Today, of almost every physical book, we know that an on-line version of it exists someplace. On-line books are even more ephemeral than paper books. Yet, they "exist" so long as the technology is available to re-present them to us. Today, the irony of old, heavy books is that thousands and thousands of books can be put on a disc or on a kindle to bypass the weight problem altogether. Yet, I wonder whether a human being can have the same pleasure in finding a book on-line as he did on accidentally discovering it in an old bookstore? Or can one's own book, library, lovingly collected over the years, be reduplicated by an on-line computer memory?

A certain comfort, I admit, is found in the fact that almost anything one publishes today can be found by some search-engine. We do not fear book-burners any more. They say that Martin Luther burnt Aristotle. Such an act today would be useless as almost anyone could find Aristotle on-line. Yet, I do worry about the governments that control systems of information. The limits they set on what cannot be "preserved" on-line may well come to the mention of God. It already does in some places.

What is the relation between a professor and his books? Obviously, the book that he writes is likely to last longer than he does. Indeed, a book in some sense is itself immortal, provided that a mind exists to know it. Most of the great writers of our kind are already dead. We can only encounter them in their books or in their still available on-line lectures. Indeed, some think that the universities themselves should be basically on-line institutions. I would think that a radical difference exists between a professor in person teaching sixty students and the same professor teaching on-line six hundred or six thousand students. Physical presence counts for something. We are not abstractions.

Old professors exist to see that old books are passed on to generations that find more reality in the future than in the past. The past is full of real people and real events. But the future, as such, contains no actual human being. This alone accounts for the charm of history. The future is populated with imagination and promises. The past is a nexus of lived lives that betray the range of human good and ill and all in-between. Old soldiers are said not to die but to fade away. Old books? Old professors? They exist, if they are worthy, to keep what is not worth losing.

Chapter 41

ON THE "MOST UTTERLY MEANINGLESS
TALK IN THE WHOLE WORLD"

A former student asked my advice about a projected academic paper on "the possibility or impossibility of becoming myself." Though much room for confusion exists in such terminology, I remarked that we are already ourselves and have so been approximately from our beginning. We cannot "become" anything or anyone else. I suppose it is proper to talk of the selves we are, as Aristotle does, "becoming" good or bad. We do have some control over whether we are praiseworthy or blameworthy. But we shall never be anything other than ourselves, good or bad.

On July 29, 1922, Chesterton tells us that he had been reading some then current novels, the gist of which contained complaints that the "modern" parent had been too kind to the children (*CW*, XXXII, 1989, 315–19). This parental niceness did not prepare the children for the cruel world, so they blamed their parents. "It seems a little hard on the late Victorian idealist," Chesterton observed, "to be so bitterly abused merely for being kind to his children." This kindly "ideal of education," moreover, was itself a reaction against the previous ideals of the parents of the Victorian idealists. The grandparents thought their children needed a little stern discipline, for which their children blamed them. So it turns out that the new novelists are in effect either "rediscovering their grandparents" or trying to concoct some third model.

These newer idealists approve of neither kindness nor discipline but "individuality." This "individuality" theory seeks to draw "out the true personality of the child" or to "allow a human being to find his real self." This terminology, it struck me, was preciously close to the request I had received from the student about the assigned project of "becoming oneself," So there is more here than at first meets the eye.

Such a project of drawing out the true personality or becoming oneself, Chesterton humorously quipped, "is perhaps *the most utterly meaningless talk in the whole muddle of the modern world.*" Even in Chesterton's terms, this "utterly meaningless talk" is a blunt rejection of what looks at first sight like a very modern and very popular position. "How is a child of seven to decide whether he has or has not found his true personality?" Chesterton asks. "Or a young man of twenty?" we might add with equal logic. "How, for that matter, is any grown-up person to tell it for him? How is anybody to know whether anybody has become his true self?" Logically, on this hypothesis, the world could be full of selves who are not themselves, as it were.

Thus, if someone should ask me, "Schall, are you, in your present wretched condition, your true self?" "Have you finally become yourself?"—what am I to respond? Am I modestly to answer: "Shucks, I am exactly what I originally planned myself to be?" Surely I do not say: "No, I am someone else. For on the way to becoming Schall, I actually became Sam Jones, who is the real Schall."

To ask such questions on such premises, Chesterton thought, is a question of "mystification." If there is a purpose in our creation, it can only be the purpose of a Creator, not of ourselves. "It can only be the purpose of God and even then it is a mystery." And if we deny that we exist because of some purpose in God, then we are in a "muddle." On the contrary, "humanly considered, a human personality is the only thing that does in fact emerge out of the combination of the forces inside the child and the forces outside." We are already persons; we deal with what happens to us.

And if we look at whether our father was kind or stern to us, how do we know which act helped and which hindered us? Most good fathers, I think, are probably both kind and stern, depends on the circumstances and what we need at the time. Such philosophers of "being ourselves" seem to think that within us some hidden being exists just waiting to jump out. Who is to tell us what does and does not help us to explain ourselves? A stern parent may in fact help as much as a kind one. And both may fail because what goes on also has something to do with what goes on inside of us.

If we examine ourselves, we are, as Chesterton thought, "influenced in some way by everything (we have) gone through." Consequently, granted this influence, "anyone would be free to speculate on what he would have been if he had never had such experiences." If someone should try to find the self minus the experiences that he has had, he "would be wasting his time." We cannot spend our lives wondering what we might have been but are not.

Any parent, Chesterton thought, knows one "simple truth." "He knows that in the most serious sense, God alone knows what the child is really like, or is meant to be really like." What can human beings do for their children, for anyone? "We can fill a child with those truths which we believe to be equally true whatever he is like. We must have a code of morals which we believe to be applicable to all children, and impose it upon the child because it is applicable to all children." Thus, if we have a little or big child who wants to be a "swindler or a torturer," we should explain to the tyke that, whatever his current preferences, we do not like these things to be done to ourselves or anyone else. And we must act on these positions.

The word "education" means to "draw out" and the word "instruction" means to "put in." There are those who often claim that what we do is "educate," not "instruct." Chesterton thinks that this latter view to be wrong because the theory on which it is based is wrong. "And I respectfully reply that God alone knows what there is to draw out; but we can be reasonably responsible for what we are ourselves putting in." We already are the persons we are from the beginning.

We become better or worse by what we do or do not do. But we do not ever make ourselves in the beginning or leave ourselves behind in the end. Whether we are punished or praised, these are things with which we have to deal. Our final personality is the result of how we deal with them, with real problems and real people, such as our parents. They either sternly rule us or look on us kindly.

Against either of these approaches, like our Victorian parents and grandparents, we can rebel, and still remain who we are, from the beginning. The "self" that we each have is given to us. "The most utterly meaningless talk in the world" is when we try to become someone else, not ourselves.

Chapter 42

ON THE *GORGIAS* MYTH

In the dialogues of Plato, we find four eschatological "myths" about what happens after death as a result of how men have lived their lives. All four stories basically teach the same thing. The shortest account is in the *Gorgias*, a dialogue of Socrates with Callicles, a suave, shrewd politician. Callicles finds it absurd to think that the politician cannot do what he wants. He holds the power of life and death. All the philosopher has to protect himself is his speech, his mind. Socrates tries to convince Callicles that his position, that "it is better to do evil than to suffer it," is wrong. He accuses Socrates of childishness, a man unable to defend himself in the real world against those with power to kill him.

Socrates' primary concern is whether the world itself is created in injustice. In this life, not all the evil deeds are punished, nor are all the good deeds rewarded. But Socrates also holds that the gods cannot be unjust. Thus, in logic, if the world *is* unjust, no gods are possible. Much is at stake.

When Socrates explains ultimate things, he often concludes with a story, an account of life after death. The teaching of the soul's immortality is a consequence of this experience. Realistic politics indicates that, frequently, the unjust are rewarded and the good punished. If this cosmic disorder is the case, surely the gods are unjust. We cannot expect anything better.

Callicles is horrified by Socrates' teaching about punishment, especially by his insistence that someone who commits a crime or sins should want to be punished. The worst thing we can do to such a man, says Socrates, is *not* to punish him. He thus continues to live a disordered life. To will to be punished is to acknowledge one's own part in the disorder. Callicles sees how this doctrine restricts the politician's power of doing what he wants. He cannot admit that some principle of what is right is stronger than this *de facto* political power to kill whomever he wants.

In the myth, in the time of Cronos, people were judged before they died. They were judged clothed so that their bare souls were obscured by prestige, money, or power. This method let those who were unjust be rewarded and those who were just unrewarded. Zeus decides to stop this injustice. Henceforth, all judgment, exercised by Minos, Radamanthus, and Aeacus, would take place after death. All would be naked so that nothing was concealed.

Radamanthus, presiding in Asia, judges Great Kings or potentates. Many crimes are stamped on their bodies and souls. "Everything was warped as a result of deception and pretense, and nothing was straight, all because the soul had been nurtured without truth" (525a–26a).

Usually, punishment justly inflicted makes men better because they see that it points to what is wrong. The wrongness, as in the similar myth in the *Phaedo*, can only be forgiven if the one against whom the crime is committed forgives.

In the *Gorgias*, the same teaching is found. In a passage hinting at the doctrine of Purgatory, we read: "Those who are benefited, who are made to pay their due by gods and men, are the ones whose errors are curable; even so, their benefit comes to them, both here and in Hades, by way of pain and suffering, for there is no other possible way to get rid of injustice." Such is indeed a remarkable passage.

Yet, in Hades, the judges find that those least likely to repent their crimes are the politicians. "From those who have committed the ultimate wrongs and who because of such crimes have become incurable come the ones who are made examples of." The doctrine of Callicles is precisely that no punishment can be requited on those who commit the great crimes.

Who commits these crimes? "The majority of these examples have come from the ranks of tyrants, kings, potentates, and those active in the affairs of cities, for these people commit the most grievous and impious errors because they're in a position to do so."

This observation suggests the link between politics and evil. This is the dilemma of Plato about whether the world is created in injustice. It does seem that the great crimes go unpunished without final judgment.

In the end, Callicles refused to discuss the matter further with Socrates. Callicles sees the logic that undermined his own position. Socrates's last words to Callicles were: "The fact is, Callicles, that those persons who become extremely wicked do come from the ranks of the powerful, although there's certainly nothing to stop good men from turning up among the powerful, and those who do turn up there deserve to be enthusiastically admitted." Politics, in its eschatological dimensions, thus remains a hazardous business. The world is not created in injustice.

Chapter 43

ON REVELATION

The word "revelation" means that something that is not known is made manifest or clear. If I maintain that nothing can be "revealed" to me, I imply either a) that I am myself omniscient or b) that nothing intelligible not already known can come to me except what is accessible to human knowledge by its own finite powers. Moreover, if something is unknown, someone or something must intervene to make it known. Otherwise, we would not know of its existence. When something becomes known, it is no longer "unknown." Once something that was not known becomes known, the new knowledge becomes the basis of further knowing even of what was already known.

If something is unknown to me, it must be made known in such a way that I can understand it. Otherwise, it is still unknown. If what I do not know is made known in Greek, then I will have to know Greek to understand what it says or have it translated into a language that I can understand. The famous or infamous phrase—"It's all Greek to me"—meant that, since I do not understand Greek, everything said in that most rational language is gibberish to me. The problem, though, is not that what is said in Greek is unintelligible, but that I do not know the language in which its intelligibility is clear.

The existence of revelation, its possibility, presupposes that many things can be known by the human mind, but not everything, or at least not without help. Revelation might mean that "contradictory" things can be known—How to square a circle sort of things. But a revelation based on this hypothesis of solving intrinsic contradictions is incoherent. That is, it could not be "revealed." It could not be a "revelation."

A revelation has to be related to mind in such a way that it does not, in making itself known, destroy the mind receiving it. Making good to be evil or impossibilities to be possible, voluntarism, in other words, destroys what-it-is-to-be-mind. If everything here and now can be other than it is, then, logically, we can know nothing. Everything that exists could be otherwise.

Catholicism is a revelation, not a religion. The word "religion" refers to a virtue by which we know what we can about God by our own human rational powers, "unaided," as they say. Revelation means that, in addition to all we know by our own powers, another source of knowledge and life exists that can address itself to us, can make itself known to us.

Some of the things that revelation makes known to us, however, we already know by our own powers. This fact is what alerts us to the persuasiveness of the other things that we do not know by our own powers. Christian revelation comes to us through the accounts of the birth, life, death, and resurrection of Christ. Its content consists of two basic elements: a) The nature of God's inner Trinitarian life, and b) One of the persons of this inner life became man. Since Christ was incarnate, He spoke to us in a human language. What He did and said could be recorded, understood, and passed down.

If these things were revealed to us, why did we need them? Why could we not figure them out by ourselves? Basically, to understand the inner life of the Godhead would require us already to be ourselves God. But if only God can understand God, it does not follow that God wants us to know nothing about His being and life.

For reasons that make sense to us, God may have wanted us to know more of what He is like than what we could figure out by ourselves. Why would God want us to know more about His own being? Because to know Him is the reason we exist in the first place.

What reasons might be given? Aquinas briefly lists four: 1) we need a clearer notion of our end, that is, of God. 2) While we can figure out many things, we need more precise notions of what is good and what is evil. 3) Most evil begins in our thoughts. We need to think clearly to act correctly. 4) We need to know if our deeds have consequences. Are they punished or rewarded? Do they mean anything? They are and they do.

Why did not God make these things so absolutely riveting that we could not help but worship Him? Basically, this move would eliminate any freedom we had. God insists that He be loved and chosen freely. His revelation bears the aura of both truth and liberty. Revelation is addressed to our minds and souls. The real drama of our existence consists in our respective responses to the divine initiative that teaches us what we are by revealing who God is.

Chapter 44

ON THE HEART OF THE DONS

Nietzsche's *Beyond Good and Evil* struck Leo Strauss as Nietzsche's "most beautiful book." This impression need not mean that it was his most "profound" book. Can something be beautiful on the outside but corrupting on the inside? By any standard, *Beyond Good and Evil*, which Nietzsche published himself selling only 118 copies, is a remarkable book. It is one of Nietzsche's last books.

The book famously affirms that Christianity, the "Platonism of the masses," is hopeless, the cause of profound weakness in society. Likewise incoherent is the philosophic endeavor of modernity to replace Christianity with some rational explanation not rooted in Plato, Aristotle, and the books of revelation. But none of these classical sources is true either.

Christians, moreover, do not live as if what they publicly profess is true. Why bother with them? "In truth, there was only one Christian," Nietzsche wrote in his *Anti-Christ*, "and he died on the Cross." Nietzsche's philosophy seems to originate as much in disappointment as in intelligence. Ultimately, he replaces reality with his own will. He calls the rest of us cowards for not going along with him.

From Nietzsche's death in 1900, to our own day, as Allan Bloom remarked, the culture has been largely ruled by Nietzsche. Power and will replaced reason and virtue as the heart of civil life. "The philosophers of the future must become the invisible spiritual rulers of a united Europe without ever becoming its servant," Strauss summed up Nietzsche's admonition (187). The invisible rulers of modern Europe, and not a few visible ones, do not want to acknowledge any Christian roots to Europe.

On reading that sentence of Strauss, we note its final phrase, "without ever becoming its (Europe's) servant." In the New

Testament, when Christ spoke of authority, He warned that it should not be exercised as "lording it" over people. In anticipation, He reversed what Nietzsche would reverse. Those who are in authority, Christ tells us, should rule as servants, not masters. The notion of rulers seeking to remain invisible but still being masters, not "servants," is frightening.

And yet, an impersonal, invisible spiritual leader who rules seems close to what is actually happening in modern democratic states. The more the people legally govern, the less they seem to be served by legal authority. Increasingly, government and its employees serve themselves, as if the end of government is the well-being of the rulers who have their own privileges by "right."

What is the origin of our disorders? Since at least Plato, it is a well-known idea that great crimes are not committed by those with IQ's low on candle-power. Hannah Arendt argued that great crimes were also committed by banal men who had nothing much to show for themselves but a kind of dogged stupidity and lethal competence.

If there is any truth in "social justice," and I think there is very little, it is that ordinary people can be blinded by lofty sounding systems of rule and eloquent demagogues. But the real problem is not usually with ordinary people. It is with what I call the "dons," clerical and academic.

The situation is paradoxical. My brother lived in a large-university town for many decades. He used to say to me after each election: "Tell me, why students in this elite university vote 95% the same way?" Generally speaking, the same way is the ideological way.

The initial answer, it seems to me, is this: "Which way do the clerical and academic dons vote?" More often than not, the one will reflect the same proportions as the other, whereas one would think, were there genuine freedom and intelligence, the results would be closer to fifty-fifty.

In Hebrews 13, we read: "Be not carried about by divers and strange doctrines." Who is most likely to be so carried about? It is ironically the "dons," intellectual and clerical, as I like to call them.

It may not be an accident that a tutor at Oxford, Italian priests, Spanish nobles, and the head of the mafia are all called "dons"!

The heart of all human disorder does not first lie in systems and organizations. It lies in the souls of men. No illusion in modern times has been more damaging than mis-locating the cause of soul-disorders in one or other aspect of societal structure.

Plato had it right from the beginning. Christianity was also correct in admonishing us first to look to our own souls. We do not like to hear this priority, I know. It seems much nobler to go forth to help others with great plans and aims that do not involve how we live and what we believe. "Seek ye first the Kingdom of Heaven," in the end, not only remains the best personal advice, but the best political advice we can have.

Chapter 45
ON SCHULZ'S "KNOWING WHAT WE KNOW NOW"

Schall is not the first to maintain that Charles Schulz of *Peanuts* fame was a first class thinker and theologian. He is easier to read than most philosophers and theologians. But that is a virtue provided one speaks the truth of things.

Linus and Sally are standing in a field. She looks at him puzzled. He observes that "Life is peculiar." In the next scene, he reflects: "Wouldn't you like to have your life to live over if you knew what you know now?" In the third frame, Sally and Linus silently look in the distance, reflecting on this profound observation. Finally, to an impassive Linus, Sally asks: "What do I know now?"

Philosophers from Aristotle to Heidegger have asked the same question—"What do I know?" "Is truth dependent on chronology?" Even with Sally's limited experience, her worries are not yet about living her life over but about getting through this one with limited knowledge.

Linus and Sally are next on a grassy field looking up at the sky. She asks: "How high are the clouds, Linus?" Linus, a scholarly sort, looking up, responds: "Oh, they're at different heights. Some of them, are 'far-away' high and some of them are 'right-up-there high," At this point, Charlie Brown appears. He was listening to this conversation. To Linus and Sally he protests: "What sort of an explanation is that?" In the last scene, Linus explains to Charlie, referring to Sally's young age: "Sometimes it's best to keep these things in the language of the layman!"

Keeping philosophy in a language that the layman could understand has been the vocation of many good philosophers. John

Paul II in *Fides et* Ratio touched on it, as does Peter Kreeft in his *Summa Philosophica*. If philosophical language is so esoteric that only a few learned souls can understand it, it is probably not very good philosophy. "What do I know?" and "How high are the clouds?" are pretty good questions. Sally isn't as dumb as she pretends. Charlie is right too. We must ask of our explanations whether they make sense.

On June 11, 1966, Charles Schulz gave the commencement address at St. Mary's College in California. This address is found in his autobiographical collection, *My Life with Charlie Brown*. Schulz noted that commencement speakers cover many topics. He recalls doing the previous year's *Peanuts* Christmas show. He wanted some way to indicate how children search for the true meaning of Christmas.

After some reflection, Schulz tells us: "I finally decided that every idea we had was an idea that really avoided the essential truth which was that the true meaning of Christmas could be found only in the Gospel according to St. Luke. So we had Linus recite those famous passages." No doubt, "avoiding" the essential truths of Christmas and of Christianity itself is a major industry. Linus seems to be almost the only person we know who can at least tell us the story. The "story" when heard, I suspect, still unsettles and uplifts many different souls.

About the world we live in, we sometimes wonder: "Who is in charge?" The world is made for man, but man is a certain kind of being. Some things he would like to see, things he thinks he ought to see, require powers not fully given to him

Linus has just informed Lucy of a scientific fact. She doesn't like it. She raises her voice: "What's this about not being able to look at the eclipse?" Linus reasonably explains to her frown: "It's very dangerous...you could suffer severe burns of the retina from infra-red rays."

That is just a fact. But Lucy, arms spread wide in protest, continues: "But what's the sense in having an eclipse if you can't look at it?" All things are visible. But an eclipse cannot be looked at. Therefore, it makes no sense to have eyes or eclipses.

In the final scene, to a dazed Linus, full of scientific information, Lucy walks away still yelling: "Somebody in production sure slipped up this time." Now it takes a dull reader not to know who is in charge of production when it comes to eclipses and eyes. From her point of view, Lucy's logic is impeccable.

Yet, behind it there is something of a rebellion against *what is*. It may well be that we are designed to know all things. Aristotle defined our mind precisely this way. Lucy is quite amusing, no doubt of it. But she is impatient about the limits. The world should be ordered to her demands. If it is not, she wants to know who is "in charge." She finds out when she listens to Linus recite the Christmas story from the Gospel of St. Luke. Yes, Schulz is a pretty good philosopher and theologian.

Chapter 46
ON REALLY LOVING THE "HAIRLESS BIPEDS"

C. S. Lewis' *Screwtape Letters* are about the ways the diabolic mind counters God's grace and truth. Robert Reilly, in his new book, *Making Gay Okay*, remarks that often we are content to lie to ourselves about *what is*, about what we do and hold. The first citation in the Reilly book is from Malcolm Muggeridge: "People do not believe lies because they have to, but because they want to." That passage pretty well sums up what the devilish mind seeks to establish in us; that is, a willingness to lie about even the most obvious truths if they go counter to what we want.

In Letter XIV, Screwtape explains to his devil apprentice how the divine mind works. The subject is humility, a high level virtue. To be humble is to acknowledge real things, including ourselves, *as they are*. But what exists in each thing is its goodness. The devil wants us to use what humility we have to call attention to ourselves, not to the thing out there which we acknowledge *as it is*. The falsely humble man, however, implicitly says "Oh, look at me," while telling everyone at the same time how unworthy he is.

The teacher devil explains that the divine mind ("the Enemy" to the devil) wants to find a truly humble man (not unlike Aristotle's magnanimous man). He is one who "could design the best cathedral in the world, and know it to be the best, and rejoice in the fact, without being any more (or less) glad at having done it than he would be if it had been designed by another." This devil is a pretty good teacher of Christianity, I must say.

"The Enemy" (that is, God) "wants each man, in the long run, to be able to recognize all creatures (even himself) as glorious and excellent things." Notice that two things are involved here: 1) a glory and excellence exist in real things, and 2) we can and ought to recognize and state this glory and excellence.

Now, what puzzles and annoys Screwtape is how "the Enemy" wants to make these human creatures, sometimes referred to as "vermin" by the devil clan, more charitable and grateful by destroying their self-love which gets in their way. This is why the diabolic policy is always to increase self-love so that everything is not seen for *what it is*, but as something that merely calls attention to oneself. Only when one of these human varmints can love his neighbor as himself can he finally figure out what it means to love himself. Each person, after all, is also a good created by God, not himself.

There was a theory, which Lewis mentions early in the book, that the reason for the hatred of the fallen angels for both God and mankind was because the angels had some sort of vision of the Incarnation. This reality meant that God became man. Not a few of the devils, led by one Lucifer, a particularly bright one, thought this was too much and rebelled.

Once they were tossed out of their original situation, these fallen angels spend their time trying to confuse and deflect human beings from achieving their own ultimate purpose which is also, with the angels, to share in the eternal inner life of the triune Godhead. Some such reasoning is probably why St. Paul told us that our main struggle is not against flesh and blood but against "principalities and powers" (Ephesians, 6:11).

Thus, Screwtape understands much of the policy of "the Enemy." He knows how He goes about guiding mankind through virtue, prayer, and truth. But Screwtape still cannot get what "the Enemy" sees in these lowly human types. To his nephew, Wormwood, he complains: "For we must never forget the most repellant and inexplicable trait in our Enemy. He really loves the *hairless biped* he has created." Somehow, I always smile when I read that description of our kind—*the hairless bipeds*. Screwtape cannot figure out how anybody, let alone God, could stoop so low.

The devil's problem, as Lewis implies, is also a lack of humility. He is unwilling to recognize the goodness in anything. This reluctance is really pride. He insists that the only good is the good he calls good, not the good that *is* good, and, on this basis, what we designate it as such.

But when God ("the Enemy") really loves the "hairless biped," He still leaves him the dignity of his freedom. He allows man not to reciprocate His love for him. Man can look squarely at the good, even his own good. He can deny that it has any origin that he needs to recognize or respond to. In the end, any given *hairless biped* is free not to recognize the good that is in himself. Though he need not, he lies to himself about himself.

Chapter 47

ON THE DEPTHS OF VILLAINY

Probably the most famous letter writer of the ancient world was Cicero. In 59 B.C., Cicero wrote to Gaius Scribonius: "There are many sorts of letters. But there is one unmistakable sort, which actually caused letter-writing to be invented in the first place, namely the sort intended to give people in other places any information which for our or their sake they ought to know." Though the letter seems to have largely been replaced by instantaneous electronic forms of communication, still we need and want to know what we "ought" to know.

Of Plato's letters, we seem to have some thirteen with various degrees of certainty about his authorship. Of these letters, the most famous is the seventh. It is a profoundly philosophic letter full of things we ought to know, things that, in many ways, remain as fresh as they day in which they were written.

Near the end of this seventh letter, Plato reflects on the reasons for Dion's failure to reform Sicily and is killed in the process. Plato was fond of Dion but, as with too many young men, he (Dion) was impatient to change the world quickly, to set up a fine regime in Sicily no matter what the raw material there with which he had to work. To help in this project is why Dion sent for Plato in the first place. Dion cajoled Plato three times into coming over from Athens to Sicily to work on Dionysius, the ruler, who, so Dion thought, had some philosophic potential. Here was Plato's chance to practice what he always preached about the best regime.

But it was not to be. Some things in human affairs can only be achieved "gradually," as Aquinas cautioned. "There is nothing surprising in what he (Dion) experienced. For although a good man who is also prudent and sagacious cannot be altogether deceived about the character of wicked men," Plato wrote;

it would not be surprising, if he should suffer the misfortune of a skillful captain, who, though not unaware of the approach of a storm, may not see its extraordinary and unexpected violence, and be swamped by its force. This is the mistake Dion made. Those who caused him to fall were men whom he well knew to be villains, but he did not suspect *the depth of their ignorance and villainy* and greed. By this error, he is fallen, and all Sicily is overwhelmed with grief" (351d).

Good men are usually not totally deceived about the "character of wicked men." The skillful politician knew of the depths of "human villainy." But still he was not expecting it when disaster happened to him.

Plato wanted to maintain that the origin of evil is largely in ignorance. If we only knew, we would be virtuous. Yet, as everyone knows, the intelligent can be wicked. Indeed, both Greek literature and Scripture teach us that the wickedest are often the most intelligent gone wrong. Socrates himself often said that we could not expect too much damage from the less gifted. It is the intelligent man gone wrong from whom we must diligently protect ourselves.

We are loathe to admit this paradox, even though we know that an element of good is found in every evil. No one can do something wrong without also doing something right. But the "what is right" is usually misplaced, deliberately so, in order to make what is wrong seem to be what is right. If, in addition, we evaporate any meaning out of things so that they have no objective standing, then right and wrong become merely "subjective."

From the side of poetry or even philosophy, it has long been assumed to be much easier to explain evil than good. When it comes to ease of explanation, however, the mystery of iniquity is no match for the mystery of the good. Lucifer indeed always makes a better stage appearance than the good angels. It is easier to explain why we steal than to explain why we do not steal. Thus, it is clear that we often do what we would not, as St. Paul expressed it. We do it to establish ourselves as the origin of what is good. And yet, we quickly discover that our own self-defined "good" clashes with *what is good*.

In Plato's *Sophist*, we read: "We need to use every argument we can to fight against anyone who does away with knowledge, understanding, and intelligence, but at the same time asserts anything at all about anything" (249c). Perhaps no passage in all of philosophy is more illuminating, more aware of the ironies of our existence. How amusing! We find that someone who subtly explains that no truth or knowledge of things is possible or desirable subsequently turns around to give us reasons why there is no reason. The man who denies the power or reason gives arguments for why he denies it.

The "villainy of evil," at bottom, is the use of reason to deny reason, to deny that there is an order to which we are open. Yet, before order, we can close our eyes and not see. It is not really that we do not see, but that we do not want to see. When we make this choice not to see or know, we cannot but give reasons for it. We contradict ourselves and invite our arguments to be tested by those who hear us give reasons.

We are often led to believe that if we lead good lives, if we seek the truth all will be well with us. Ultimately, this is true. Yet, as Plato taught us, especially in the second book of the *Republic*, even the best and wisest of men will probably be exposed to the "villainy of evil" precisely because they are good. Brought to this realization, we are left a choice to accept or reject the basic Socratic dictum that "It is never right to do wrong," especially in the face of such villainy that we too often encounter in this world.

Ultimately, this confrontation is why it is more difficult to explain what is good than to explain what is evil. The explanation of evil always involves putting ourselves first over against what is good. In the end, the explanation of the good includes the overcoming of evil by what is not evil, not by what is evil. This is why Socrates uses the prophetic word "suffer."

The "villainy of evil" always ends in attacking what is good because it is good. Even wise and prudent men sometimes, perhaps often, forget this ongoing struggle that, more than anything else, defines the real affairs of men in this world. All of this, as Cicero implied in his letter to Gaius, tells us about things we ought to know, things that the letters of Plato spell out with more clarity and detail than we are used to seeing even today, especially today.

Chapter 48
ON THE PHILOSOPHY FOUND ON SPORTS' PAGES

The best writing in newspapers is found on the sports' page. But I am not concerned with "good writing" but with "philosophy." The sports' pages reveal the drama of winning and losing, of cheating and playing by the rules. They deal with the Platonic problem of constantly changing the rules so that the game grandsons play is not the same game grandfathers played. Rules and equipment changes have made records over time incomparable. Plato said that changes in regime are first indicated by changes in music and games.

Still, changes in rules may be positive. Sally Jenkins, in *The Real All Americans* (W. *Post*, May 13, 2000), about the Carlisle Indians, tells us that "the first downfield, overhand spiral (pass) was completed on Sept. 5, 1906, when St Louis quarterback Bradbury Robinson threw to teammate Jack Schneider in an obscure game against Carroll College." Today, football games seem to be at least half passes. The first forward pass did not evidently come in a Notre Dame game but with the Carlisle Indians. Both "obscurity" and "fame" are found on the fields of play.

High Greek drama is found on the sports' page—the heroic father, the prancing son, and the alien step-mother. NASCAR driver Dale Earnhardt Jr. was a popular driver. His famous father had been killed on the last lap of the Indianapolis 500. After some years driving for his father's racing company, next operated by his step-mother, young Earnhardt decided to go with another racing outfit. This family controversy became at the time the talk of the racing industry.

Here is how Liz Clarke described the situation (*Washington Post*, May 13, 2007): "Only recently had it become public knowledge that his (Earnhardt, Jr.) relationship with his step-mother, Teresa Earnhardt, who took control of the team following her husband's death, was strained at best. The difference was that their discord was played out in the national media rather than behind closed doors." This drama is now out there for everyone to contemplate. Normal clods play their tragic dramas unnoticed.

What was the lesson? "The Earnhardts simply added their name to the long list of American family dynasties—whether built on oil, newspapers, hotel chains, or sports teams –riven by money, power, ego and enmity." The key verb is "riven." This is straight Sophocles and Augustine. The doom of the gods is on the heroes of our kind.

If someone has never seen *Oedipus Rex* or *King Lear*, no matter. It's there for us to contemplate with our morning coffee— *"money, power, ego, and enmity."* The explanation is in the first book of Aristotle's *Ethics*. Our aristocracies have, besides politics, other titles to glory or disaster.

The horse I bet on in the Kentucky Derby one year was named Hard Spun, only my nephew never got the email announcing my $2 bet, paid by him. The horse was trained by Larry Jones. Jones wore a distinctive white western hat. His training habits were not considered orthodox. Hard Spun was put through a fast exercise race against a fast filly with the wonderful name, "Wildcat Bettie B," a few days before the Derby. Jones seemed, as the great race writer, Andrew Beyer, put it "indecisive" about even running the horse in the Derby. Jones was subject to a lot of criticism. Hard Spun's jockey, Mario Pino, had a reputation for coming in second in big races.

Hard Spun led all the way to the end when the favorite Street Sense caught him. Still Hard Spun beat eighteen other thoroughbreds. Jones proved that he knew what he was about. "After the Derby, the Associated Press quoted him (Jones): 'I think I think more than y'all think I think'" (*Washington Post*, 14 May). And that is also my final word on the philosophy of reading the sports page: "I think I think more thinking occurs there than on the pages where thinking is reputed to be thinking, but 'ain't.'"

Chapter 49

ON NATURAL RESOURCES

In Psalm 8, we read: "You have given him (man) rule over the works of your hands, putting all things under his feet." This passage recalls the "dominion" passage in Genesis (1:28). It means that the natural resources of the earth and cosmos are given to man so that, through them, he can live and attain his purposes. This view is teleological. It finds that, discernable within the cosmos, things relate to each other. Each order of existing things, by being what it is, has a purpose. This abiding uniqueness of existing things is why we can study and know them with our minds. All non-human purposes are, by being good, themselves ordered to the purpose of man. It follows that, if we do not know both the inner-worldly and transcendent purpose of man, we do not know the purpose of the things we find in the universe.

I approach these comments on natural resources from a specific angle. Today, the world is not understood to be "for" man, but man is "for" the world. This deliberate reversal of the hierarchy of ends within the natural order means that the chief interest of man is not his own soul. It is rather the presumed carrying capacity of the earth, and perhaps the cosmos itself. The "species" counts, not John or Suzie, who can be expendable. The "future" means, not eternal life, but the temporal on-going of the planet down the ages. Salvation means "saving" the planet, usually from some men for the good of presumed others yet to appear. In this context, estimates (and that is all that they are) of resource availability become the principal concern of men and states. Ethics becomes the "engineering" of this saving of some men through allocation of resources.

Talk of "rights" of trees or sparrows belongs to the same discourse of human "rights," when "rights" mean whatever we want them to mean. "Rights" do not refer to something intrinsic to the being in question. Rather, as Hobbes said, they are whatever we want to make of them. We can endow "rights" on turtles but not on babies in the womb. This "liberty" is what "rights" are designed to accomplish.

We look to the "future" of the planet. Human beings are considered its greatest threat. They use "natural" resources. They must be controlled for future generations. We control them by postulating a "scarcity" of natural resources. This supposed lack obliges us to distribute what is left "fairly." No previous political thinker, not even Machiavelli, devised a better "presupposition" on which to base absolute power over ordinary human beings than this presumed "scarcity" of goods down the ages.

But what's the problem here? Are not resources finite? Do we not need to "protect" the environment? If we inquired of a learned man in A.D. 1800, or even 1500 B.C., whether the planet could support a population of some seven billion human beings as it does today, he would not see how it was possible. Why would he not see it? He could not imagine that human intelligence could devise ways to use what is given in the Earth's resources for the good of so many people. Such ancestors might, however, understand that such human beings, if they did come to exist centuries later, might still have the basic human problems and have the same human destiny as themselves.

In terms of natural resources, the planet is adequate for the purposes that God had for it. Evidently, these resources were not simply to be left unused by each successive generation. It turns out, moreover, that the availability of resources is itself subject to the human mind's understanding of them. This is why politics based on their presumed scarcity are themselves self-fulfilling. They rest on the assumption that our knowledge and capacity will be pretty much as they are now. And since we presume that we can anticipate what existing human beings in five hundred, a thousand, or two thousand years hence (if we last that long) might need, we base our present assumption of scarcity on what is in effect a myth.

Man himself is a "natural resource." He exists on this planet from nature like everything else. He is different because he has a mind. This mind is the one anti-entropic power within the universe that sees what is there, what he is. The real natural resource is his mind in which what is not himself is known and placed in order. The hallmark of the universe is not scarcity but abundance. Man's "dominion" makes it possible for natural resources to reach their end. Man alone is the cosmic "natural resource" that must choose to accept his own end. The real drama of the universe lies with the "natural resource" that is man.

Chapter 50
ON THE LOGIC OF DENYING
"INTELLIGENT DESIGN"

Usually, spotting an automobile bearing more than one bumper sticker raises the eyebrows. Recently, I noticed a parked car with a bumper sticker that read: "I'm Already Against the Next War." I thought "Give me liberty or give me death" is not part of this man's vocabulary. If we needed him in the next crisis, he would not be around.

The man of this persuasion would logically acquiesce in whatever happens. He would think himself virtuous in so doing. He would maintain his "principle." What at first sounded like high mindedness, when spelled out, is cowardice. The consequence of the slogan relies on someone else to keep him free. He does nothing to protect himself or others. Yet, he demands praise for his nobility in doing nothing to prevent terrible evils.

By chance, the same car, with the stickers all over it, appeared again. They were visible and intended to be. A new sticker not seen before affirmed: "Intelligent Design Is Neither." Had I looked on the same car, I could probably find "Earth Warming" signs and an Obama sticker.

"Intelligent Design Is Neither." This statement is intended to be "intelligent." That is, the sloganeer assumes that meaning is found in the statement. He intends its intelligence, what it says, to be intelligible to any reader, whoever he be, even Schall.

But can such a proposition, as it stands, properly have a "meaning," given the validity of the initial proposition? In other words, is the statement intrinsically contradictory to itself so that its very affirmation constitutes a denial of the proposition as stated?

Current controversy over "Intelligent Design" goes to the heart of modern relativism. Benedict XVI used the expression in this regard. The notion of "intelligent design" is found in Aquinas' proofs for the existence of God.

Denying that an intelligent design is found in nature protects us against any claim that the human being, through his mind, is ordered to something beyond himself. No "proof" for intelligence or design, it is claimed, can be known through the mind's knowing of what is not itself, through its knowing of what designed the world "intelligently."

At issue is whether chance and order are contradictory to each other. Yet, when spelled out, the intelligibility of chance itself, insofar as it has any, indicates purpose. Chance is when two purposeful things, doing what they do to achieve their purpose, cross each other. The question of God or an omniscient knower is whether even chance is or can be reduced to order, such that chance events also belong to the providential order of things.

Again: "Intelligent design is neither." Neither what? It is neither a) intelligent, nor is it b) a design. The world exists not by "intelligent design" but, so to speak, by "non-intelligent" "non-design," by chaotic disorder. Or put in the same form: "Non-intelligent non-design is both." That proposition would mean that "non-intelligent non-design is intelligent." That is, to the holder of the thesis that denies any intelligibility in the world, it is "intelligent" to say that no intelligence or design is found.

With these paradoxes, what is now the issue? Where did this "intelligence," whereby we deny intelligence and design, come from? If it "evolved," was it intended to evolve? Logically, in the next evolution, it could mean its opposite. That is, what is now "intelligent" could be "non-intelligent." Thus, intelligent and non-intelligent would mean the same thing, unless we presupposed something lying outside the non-intelligent, non design system. But by virtue of the principle, such a "something" that explains the system should not exist.

The proposition that "Intelligent design is neither" brings us back from the universe in which intelligent design may or may not exist to our own minds. We happily use our minds to decide whether it makes sense to find or deny some design or order in the universe. It is one thing to say "Intelligent design is neither." It is another thing to say that this proposition can mean anything unless some stable intelligence and design do exist that make it worth our while to state the proposition to other human beings.

The man who concocted the slogan thought that it would reinforce the case of those who deny intelligence and design in the universe and, hence, in human beings. He forgot that, in his very denial, "design" and "intelligibility" were presumed in his mind. Otherwise, as in the case of Zeno, I believe, he would have had to shut up.

Whatever the scientific case for intelligent design may or may not be, it makes no sense to try to convince Schall that no intelligibility and no design are found if the statement designed to show this incoherence appeals to his intelligence. Intelligence itself is designed to make us understand something. Using intelligence to deny intelligence is not intelligent.

Chapter 51

ON THE TYRANT

Repeatedly reading Greek and Roman thought makes certain figures more vivid. Who is the philosopher? Who is the statesman? The tyrant is always among the most important to understand. In one way or another, he appears in most Platonic dialogues. Aristotle describes him, as do Thucydides and Xenophon.

What initially surprises people reading of the tyrant is that he is not an ugly, deformed brute. Callicles is not repulsive, but sophisticated, a college man. Alcibiades is among the most charming of young Greeks. The tyrant is in fact quite clever, witty, usually handsome and affable, always eloquent.

What else strikes us as odd is that the tyrant almost invariably arises out of a democracy. Democracy breeds tyrants. We are loathe to hear it. But we are also reluctant to examine the guiding spirit of the actual regimes we designate as "democratic."

A democracy is a regime in which "freedom" rules. Here "freedom" is defined, not as allowing us to follow what is virtuous, but the relativist permission to do whatever we will. The democratic regime makes no judgment about right or wrong. As a result, right and wrong are defined by the polity, from which no appeal is permitted. Nothing is higher than civic will.

A regime in which anyone can do whatever he wills has no standards. It soon swerves about aimlessly like the ship in Plato's *Republic* VI. The young tyrant sees that no one stands for anything. He conceives himself as the savior to order this social chaos. His own empty soul is motivated by fame as much as by power. He wants everyone to think and say that he "does good," whatever he does.

At the end of *Republic* I, Socrates broaches the question: Is the tyrant the happiest of men? He can command whatever he wants.

He surrounds himself with those who will do his will, tell him what they think he wants. He begins to have "body guards." Not only is he "happy" because he can command what he wants, but, even more subtly, he can order everyone else to his private happiness. His good is the common good. All are ordained to him and praise him.

When we come to the end of *Republic* IX, we see that the tyrant, who uses everyone else for his own purposes, turns out to be, not the happiest of men, but the unhappiest. He can trust no one. Every relationship with him is tainted with fear or false adulation. Like Nero in the description of Tacitus, no one dares to contest with him in any field.

Yet, as Aristotle remarks, the tyrant wants to be loved. He craves public admiration. He arranges many public appearances. He wants people to tell him that he is nobly serving them. Of course, love is not the proper relation of ruler to ruled. Justice is. The confusion of love and rule was pictured by Allan Bloom in the case of King Lear. He wanted something beyond politics, love for him, to be a political test.

The dialogues of Plato are filled with promising young men who come to Socrates to learn how to rule. Socrates is coy with them. Their souls are disordered. They want power without discipline or insight. They want to learn to speak persuasively. They want to sound good, not be good.

The tyrant only hears what he wants to hear. A tyrant must prevent friendships among the people, Aristotle noted. Friendships imply something beyond the tyrant's control. But the tyrant has no real friends of his own. He cannot tell why people surround him. He is not sure of the advice he is given. He only hears what people think he wants to hear. The tyrant becomes more and more isolated. He cannot go out in public without his body guards. He is essentially alone.

The tyrant acknowledges nothing higher than himself. Still, the tyrant himself wisely leads an ascetic life, no drinking and carousing, as brutal tyrants do. Everything must be public. People must be kept busy, stimulated. They must build pyramids; they must be kept employed preferably beholden to the tyrant's regime.

The modern tyrant has the advantage not only of being in control of the military but of the means of communication. Though the tyrant rules for his own sake, he insists that his rule is beneficial to everyone. Only traitors have any criticism of him. Nothing transcendent is allowed. No judge exists but himself of his own actions.

Tyrants can last a long time. People adjust to tyrannical rule. Their souls become lethargic. The tyrant often dies in bed, much admired. The souls of citizens reflect the configuration of the polity. The tyrant has taken the measure of freedom. Tyrants are safe so long as, in their souls, people define freedom as the doing of whatever they want.

Chapter 52

ON SALVATION

Newt Gingrich once predicted that God would be legally driven out of public life in the United States. James Hitchcock's book, *The Supreme Court and Religion in American Life*, recalls the various "conscientious objection" cases in which the "Supreme Being," in which one had sincerely to believe for exemption, was expanded to mean "belief in and devotion to goodness and truth for their own sake," or "belief in religion in an ethical sense." Just what it was one believes becomes ever fuzzier.

People often attest that they have and need no "belief." They just lead "good lives." The self-delusions of belief and good lives are legendary. Modern ecumenical and liberal modes hesitate to condemn anyone for anything. The belief that everyone is saved is much more prevalent than the view that some are lost. Logically, if few or many are lost, not everyone is saved.

In an All Souls' Day sermon entitled, delightfully, "Because Non-Smokers Die Too," George Cardinal Pell remarked: "If the belief flourishes that everything is forgiven—that everyone goes to heaven—even without repentance—this soon translates to being uncertain whether anyone goes to heaven, or whether there is any Godly forgiveness beyond the human forgiveness of the victims" (*Be Not Afraid*, 253). Evidently, the distinction between the saved and the damned is not equivalent to that between smokers and non-smokers! Efforts to keep us from smoking are more high-pressured than those designed to keep us from sinning.

I bring these topics up because, I chanced to re-read a famous passage in *Lumen Gentium*, Vatican II's document on the Church. The recent popes have stressed the need for evangelization. Yet this admonition comes at a time when, both because of civil disabilities against any proselytism in many countries and because of doubt about whether it is needed, the zeal to evangelize seems wanting.

Salvation means that we accept Jesus Christ as the Lord. It means living a life worthy of our calling. It means repenting our sins. Yet, we read in *Lumen Gentium*: "God's plan of salvation embraces those also who acknowledge the Creator." Evidently, this clarification is designed to distinguish them from those who acknowledge the Redeemer. "Among these (acknowledging the Creator) are especially the Mohammedans; they profess their faith as the faith of Abraham, and with us they worship the one, merciful God who will judge men on the last day." This is a remarkably benign view of Islam which positively rejects the notion of Trinity and Incarnation as contrary to Allah and, in recent years, contributes many Christian martyrs to the list of saints.

The Document recalls St. Paul in Athens: "God himself is not far from those who seek the unknown God in darkness and shadows, for it is he who gives to all men life and inspiration and all things, and who as Savior desires all men to be saved." Obviously, this group would include those who seek goodness and truth, whatever they mean. It appears that honorable seeking is enough.

Further, "eternal salvation is open to those who, through no fault of their own, do not know Christ and his Church but seek God with a sincere heart, and under the inspiration of grace try in their lives to do his will, made known to them by the dictates of their conscience." Grace is seen working outside the visible confines of the Church, but not apart from the Spirit's being sent into the world. Like the Court, the Church here insists that the person holding these positions must be sincere and in a position of unavoidable ignorance about the truth of revelation. Suicide bombers usually meet this criterion.

Finally, Divine Providence does not "deny aids necessary for salvation to those who, without blame on their part, have not yet reached an explicit belief in God, but strive to lead a good life, under the influence of God's grace." By such criteria, one wonders who, other than a few unrepentant believers, are not saved. If the vast majority are going to be saved with these beliefs, why disturb them?

One wonders whether there are more erroneous consciences than we are led to believe exist in the world, or whether the objective order is not more demanding than we suspect.

Chapter 53

ON LUCK

In his 1906 book on Algeria, *Esto Perpetua*, Belloc meets a French-man there. He asked him if he thought himself "prosperous." "He said, as do all sad people, that luck was the difference." Why were the luckless called "sad"? It is, I suppose, because, when the dice do not roll our way, no one can be blamed for our plight. A statistical order exists in the rolling of the dice. The flip of a coin—if the coin does not fall our way, if we did not "luck" out—is just the way it is—sad.

The words, *luck, chance, accident,* and *fortune,* all have the same meaning. At first sight, no specific "cause" of luck or chance can be identified. No one is to blame. That is why it can be used "reasonably." To choose who is to kick and who is to receive in a football game, the only "fair" way is to employ chance. Once the first step is decided, the second step, in fair play, gives the next priority to the loser. Without the rational agreement to abide by chance, we could not begin "fairly." Yet, to be the "lucky" winner of a lottery, say, has its rewards—the proverbial "luck of the Irish."

Luck appears in Scripture. In Acts, Matthias was chosen by lot over Joseph Barsabbas to replace Judas among the Twelve (1:23). The United States and other countries today have hundreds of casinos whose basic business, when honest, is luck and its fascination. We work hard to "beat the odds."

We sometimes underestimate the influence of chance in our lives. Indeed, we wonder if many things that seem to be results of accident or chance are not somehow "intended." As far as I can ascertain, every existing human being is, at first sight, the result of chance. The first meeting of one's father and mother was to all appearances, a chance, a blind date, an unexpected trip, a girl next door. Yet, we also say that each of us is "intended" by God from the beginning. If this intention is so, something more than chance is at work in chance. Chance itself needs to be reduced to order. More or less, this is what providence is about.

In discussing chance in *A General Theory of Authority*, Yves Simon explained the "rationality" of irrational accidents. Millions of road "accidents" happen every year. Purpose exists in accidents. Each driver is going to a certain place for a reason. Neither driver in an accident intended to run into the other. So chance occurs when two reasonable actions cross outside the purpose of either.

But accidents have consequences, often dire ones. Most people know someone in the family or neighborhood who was injured or killed in an accident. We try to fix the blame on someone or something. It "should" not have happened, yet it did. We have to live with accidents. Our insurance economy is based on dealing with the "sad" things that bad luck brought about. Insurance is a way to spread out the cost of accidents.

And the rise and fall of nations? Is that due to luck, fortune? Belloc was in the ruins of the ancient Roman-African city of Timgrad. There he chanced to meet a man "of a kind I had not encountered before." "We discussed together in these brief moments the chief business of mankind." The man knew something of Sussex, Belloc's native county in England. He told Belloc that, in the desert, the stars were "terrible to man" and "the distances endless."

This remark caused Belloc to remember "the old knowledge"— namely, "How great nations as they advance with unbroken records and heap up experience, and test life by their own past, and grow to judge exactly the enlarging actions of men, see at last that there is no Person in destiny, and that purpose is only in themselves. Their faiths turn to legend, and at last they enter into that shrine whose God has departed and whose Idol is quite blind."

Destiny is chance, not purpose. Purpose is in ourselves. What we sometimes call "fate" is really the plan of God, a plan that free men can reject. We are tempted to look back at our lives to think that they "must" have happened the way that they did. We thus think that the world is made only of chance with no purpose. If so, we have no responsibility for it.

And what is the "chief business of mankind"? It is to see that "purpose is only in ourselves." Even if we meet by chance, we choose by judgment. No reason can be given why a world of pure chance would exist. It would be a shrine of a departed God, a blind Idol. But a world in which both chance and purpose exist together is quite likely. Such is a world in which the results of both luck and choice exist with real effects on our lives and world.

Chapter 54
ON BEING A BASEL PROFESSOR

In Walter Kaufmann's chronology of Nietzsche's life, under 1889, it states briefly, that "Nietzsche becomes insane early in January in Turin."

Insanity, evidently, is no impediment to writing letters. Chesterton said that the maniac was the man with the one idea that explains everything. He is the completely rational man for whom everything made sense in terms of his one idea. It does no good to tell the man who thinks that he is Napoleon that he is *not* Napoleon. For if he were Napoleon and someone told him that he was not, he would be certain that the other person, not himself, was mad, since he knows he is Napoleon. The madman sees himself first and everything else in terms of himself.

Nietzsche is the most amusing of the philosophers, except perhaps for Chesterton himself. This series, "On Letters and Essays" (in *University Bookman*), is, in its own way, an homage to the wonderful existence of letters and essays in our literary tradition. Some of the finest things we ever read or write are in our short letters or essays. And, of course, with his aphorisms and maxims, Nietzsche is a master of philosophic brevity and wit.

In *The Wanderer and the Shadow*, Nietzsche himself, in an age when letters were, as it were, still letters, not e-mails, wrote: "A letter is an unannounced visit; the mailman, the mediator of impolite incursions. One ought to have one hour every eight days for receiving letters, and then take a bath" (#261, *Portable Nietzsche*). I presume this advice was not intended for us to take one of those invigorating baths just to relax and enjoy the warm water. "Unannounced visits" are often the best kind. I suspect Nietzsche saw them as intrusions into his own world that he claimed to dominate with his will.

On January 6, 1889, just when insanity was evidently setting in, from Turin, Nietzsche wrote to his famous mentor, Jacob Burckhardt. Nietzsche began, "In the end, I would much rather be *a Basel professor* than God." One suspects that God, not to mention the rest of us, would also prefer that Nietzsche be a Basel professor. The authority and prestige of German professors are, of course, legendary. We are not quite sure, with this amusing preference, whether Nietzsche is yet insane. He gives his reasoning: "I have not dared to push my private egoism so far as to desist for its sake from the creation of the world." There is self-insight and humor here.

Naturally, to recall Chesterton's maniac, a man who thought he was God would, of course, be busy creating the world. This was one of the divine occupations. To be a Basel professor, however high a preference over the divinity, might distract him from this "god's" activities. Nietzsche justifies his choice: "You see, one must make sacrifices however and wherever one lives." Lucky for us, we continue to exist even though Basel loses a professor.

Nietzsche tells Burckhardt that he has a student's room across from the Palazzo Carignano. He next claims that he (Nietzsche) was actually born in this Palazzo as Vittorio Emanuele himself. This is quite a come-down from his previous creative status! But there is music below in the Galleria Subalpina. The room only costs twenty-two francs. He does his own shopping, but has "torn shoes."

Nietzsche figures that, evidently on account of his sins, if not, more likely, his own aphorisms, he is "sentenced to while away the next eternity with bad jokes." There could be worse fates. But he has his writing with him. "The post office is five steps from here, so I mail my letters myself to play the great *feuilletonist* of the *grande monde*." This "romance writer" of the great world has some relationship with *Le Figaro* in Paris, but he wants to prove his harmlessness with two jokes.

In the first "joke," if it can be called that, Nietzsche identifies himself with two well-known criminals at the time. He wants to show Paris something which it had not seen before, namely, "a decent criminal." The second "joke" is a salute to Alphonse Daudet, who had just published a satire on the "Forty Immortals" of the French Academy, for which Nietzsche thinks he merits immediate membership in this august body.

Is Nietzsche already mad? He seems almost too witty to be so. He claims next to be "every historical personage," no mean feat, though a logical consequence of his superman position. And of the children he has "brought into the world," again back to theology, he ponders "with some misgiving the possibility that not everyone who enters the 'kingdom of God' also comes *from* God." Scripture itself says that "not everyone who says to me 'Lord, Lord,' will enter the kingdom of heaven."

But we suspect that Nietzsche has something more sinister in mind. If there is in fact someone in the Kingdom of God who is not originally "from" God, we have implicitly a denial of the creation account in Genesis in which God saw that all being was good because He created it. If Nietzsche is busy creating the world himself, instead of being a Basel professor, this is probably who slips in. He continues by telling us that he has witnessed his own funeral twice, once in the form of the natural son of the Piedmont king and once as the Papal Secretary of State.

Nietzsche next tells Burckhardt that he wants him to see what he is writing, but he may not "profit from it," because "we artists are incorrigible." He invites Burckhardt to come down to Turin for "a really fine chat." He promises "a glass of Veltliner" (a famous Austrian wine) and advises him not to worry about dressing up. Burckhardt does come down to take him back to Basel for treatment.

This famous letter has a number of postscripts on the margins. They are again rather funny. He explains that he goes about Turin in a student coat slapping some startled gentleman on the back to ask him whether "he is content?" He explains to the man that he is God, not the Papal Secretary of State. He created this "farce of a world." The reaction of the Italian gentleman to this divine slap on the back is not recorded. *Allora.*

Evidently still in his divine capacity, Nietzsche adds: "I had Caiphas put in chains; I too was crucified last year in a long, drawn-out way by German doctors. Wilhelm, Bismark and all anti-Semites done away with!" He carries out his own incarnation.

Two days before the above letter, Nietzsche wrote another letter from Turin to the composer Peter Gast that simply said: "Sing me a new song: the world is transfigured and all the heavens are full of joy." These words are obviously inspired by scripture. However, the signature is simply "the Crucified." The irony and paradox here are obviously intended. Yet, I sometimes think that Nietzsche did somehow believe his own aphorism that read: "The last Christian died on the Cross." That is why the Crucifixion haunted him, even his own, even perhaps in madness.

The man who would rather be a "Basel professor than God" was busy creating the world, his world. After we create our own world, we have to live in it. The only escape from such madness is into a world that we did not create, one that we discover already created for us, one in which we are freed from the prison of our own reason revolving creatively about itself alone.

Chapter 55
ON THE ALTERNATIVE TO HUMANITY

Josef Pieper's 1954 book, *The End of Time*, began with two citations. The second selection is from the German poet, Konrad Weiss. It reads: "The will, which is today growing ever greater, to create a condition that shall hold within it an exemplarily complete essence of humanity and an enduring peace, is burdened by the heavy paradox that it is not humanity which is the goal of the Incarnation." Weis speaks of a "will" that grows stronger. This "will" wants to gain control of all of humanity. Once it accomplishes this incorporation, we will have "peace." Man and only man will be in charge of man. But exactly whose "will" seeks these things? Evidently, for Weiss, it is not the "will" that was responsible for the Incarnation. In other words, shades of Augustine, we have two conflicting wills at work among us. Each seeks to clarify and complete *what man is*.

The Incarnation means that God becomes not "humanity" but this man, Christ, born of a woman, in a definite time and place. "Humanity" is an abstraction from an abstraction—*Socrates-man-humanity*. Humanity is not "born"; it is a mental form, valid for what it is. Humanity includes all men in one concept without necessarily identifying any individual person. Marx called it "the species-man." Weiss was correct in thinking that these two understandings are opposed to each other.

The understanding of man that flows from the Incarnation knows that *what it is to be man* is a given. "Politics does not make man to be man," Aristotle rightly said, "but taking him from nature as already man, makes him to be good man." Some minds refuse to understand man as "already man" without their input. This "no given nature" becomes the modern presupposition of liberty—

nothing there but what I will. In other words, *what it is to be man* is not taken as a given. Indeed, the idea, that *what it is to be man* is a given, is conceived to be a threat against "humanity." Why is this?

I write in the light of recent Supreme Court decisions which, at bottom, are motivated by this "will" to make man, by positive law, something other than he is by nature. The "mind" of the justices may, at first sight, seem to be their own. But they further a "will" that they do not acknowledge. This will is connected to an intelligence that "knows" what it does, an intelligence that hates man as given. The modern mind is in position to do this refashioning of man both because of modern thought and modern technology.

Weiss's wording was perceptive. This modern "will" demands "the complete essence of humanity." That is, it does not allow any possibility for an understanding of *what man is* other than its own willed formulation of it. It wants to remove not only the idea that a proper and superior understanding of *what man is* exists, but it seeks to forbid any speaking of this alternative. The "hate-language" that we see increasingly applied with regard to the content of revelation is no accident. The "complete essence of humanity" allows no alternative to its own agenda. It insists on producing a mankind closed to any signs of Incarnation that might lead us to a proper understanding of man.

In his new book, *On the God of Christians (and on one or two others),* the French philosopher Rémi Brague writes: "What is personal in us sins by rejecting living out of personal liberty and by seeking to possess what in us is natural" (63). It strikes me that this "to seek to possess in us what is natural" is Weiss' concern about the will to define and thus to control the "essence of humanity." Our political classes see themselves as free to recreate man over against *what he is* because no understanding of man is admitted except as a vague concept whose content needs to be filled in by man, not discovered from nature as already given.

This "will" that "grows" to create a better humanity than the one given in nature and confirmed by the Incarnation must logically seek, step by step, to affirm as "good" each act and way of life that was seen to be bad in nature. Thus, the content of the new humanity does not really come from man but from its opposition to whomever it was that formulated *what it is to be man* in the first place.

The "heavy paradox" of the Incarnation is indeed a "burden" that the new humanity bears since it can never really deal with ordinary human beings and their transcendent destiny but only, beginning with love and the family, recast them in forms that are directly oppose to that incarnate being in which alone man's ultimate good can be found.

Chapter 56

ON THE LIBERAL EDUCATION OF READING
LORD PETER WIMSEY

To be liberally educated is to practice Dorothy Sayers' "Lost Tools of Learning." But it is not in this famous essay alone that Miss Sayers' fame resides.

At Christmas, my sister had several books for me to read. One was Sayers' Lord Peter Wimsey detective novel entitled *Clouds of Witness*, with the sub-title: *The Solution of the Riddlesdale Mystery with a Report of the Trial of the Duke of Denver for Murder."*

The first chapter was entitled, "With Malice Aforethought." It began with a citation from *Othello*—"Oh, who hath done this deed?" The chapter ended: "Guided by these extremely plain hints, the jury, without very long consideration, returned a verdict of willful murder against Gerald, Duke of Denver." That seemed to settle it. But this was only a jury of inquiry. The real trial was yet to come.

As we quickly learn, the Duke was the brother of Lord Peter Wimsey. Moreover, his and the Duke's sister, Lady Mary, were involved. This murder was a Wimsey family affair as their Dowager mother was also present. At one point Lady Mary confessed to having murdered her fiancé, the victim, in order to protect her lover. I will not further reveal the intricate plot. In the end, the Duke was found innocent. In fact, no murder occurred but that is the plot.

Why the novel was called *Clouds of Witness* puzzled me. "Witness" is singular, not plural. Many suspects and witnesses were examined. Initially, I thought that it was about the confusion caused by conflicting testimonies. But if "witness" in the title is singular, which it is, it could mean the obscurity that still hangs over a case when all the evidence is in while things remain "cloudy."

While reading Dorothy Sayers, we are in erudite British company which somehow frequently use "ain't." When we see the word "ain't" in an American novel, like Wendell Berry's *A Place in Time*, well that's how some Kentucky folks talk. But among English aristocracy, we are pretty sure that they do not talk this way. Everyone understands that it is a deliberate affectation.

Chapter Three is entitled "Mudstains and Bloodstains." A citation from *David Copperfield* introduces it: "'Other things are all very well in their way, but give me Blood....' We say, 'There it is! There's Blood!' It is an actual matter of fact. We point it out. It admits of no doubt.... We must have Blood, you know.'" All detective story essentials are present—facts, clues, real blood, deception, and evidence.

But after a chapter in which facts and blood figure prominently, erudition comes out. Lord Peter had unearthed some evidence that seemed to favor his brother Gerald, the Duke. Lord Peter sat on a low stonewall to muse about what he had learned. "'Things began to look a bit more comfortable for old Jerry,' said Lord Peter. He... began whistling softly but with great accuracy, that elaborate passage of Bach which begins 'Let Zion's children.'" That is Bach's Motet #225: "Let us sing a new song to the Lord." This reference to Psalms 149 and 150 occurs in the middle of a detective story, whistled "with great accuracy"!

English detective novels often have something French about them. Chapter Five is entitled: "The *Rue St. Honoré* and the *Rue de la Paix*." It too is introduced by a famous reference, this time from *H. M. S. Pinafore* that reads: "I think it was the cat." The "cat" turns out to be a piece of jewelry found near the scene of the crime, but purchased in Paris by the victim for a lady.

The English detective friend of Lord Peter is Charles Parker. He is sent to Paris to check on things, especially jewelry sales. What he finds out, he writes in a letter to Lord Peter. He gives the letter to the *valet de chamber* to mail *colis postal* to England.

The next sentence reads: "After which (mailing) he (Parker) went to bed and read himself to sleep with a Commentary on the Epistle to the Hebrews." Where else but in Dorothy Sayers could we find an English police officer in Paris who goes to sleep by reading, not the Epistle to the Hebrews itself, but a commentary on it!

In reading Lord Peter Wimsey, we are liberally educated. We learn not only of murderous plots but of Shakespeare, Dickens, Gilbert and Sullivan, Bach, the last two Psalms, *and*, not least, commentaries on the Epistle to the Hebrews.

At Mass recently, the first reading was Hebrews 12:1. There it was: "A cloud of witnesses!" And the next day I received Father George Rutler's new book entitled, sure enough, *Cloud of Witnesses*. Suddenly the title of Sayers' book was not such a mystery. The police officer reading a commentary on Hebrews—what else would he read! To read a detective story, it helps to know scripture and English literature.

Chapter 57

On Giving Reasons

While reading Scripture or other sources like Aquinas, Plato, or even P. G. Wodehouse, we often have to stop and think. Previously, we may have read this or that passage several times. Yet, on re-reading it, we realize that we did not grasp what it really said. For instance, I was reading in the Breviary a passage from the tenth chapter of Paul's Second Letter to the Corinthians. This is what he said: "We demolish sophistries and every proud pretension that raises itself against the knowledge of God; we likewise bring every thought into captivity to make it obedient to Christ." We are here reminded of Plato's intense dislike of the sophists. A sophist is someone, usually learned, who uses reason to obscure or undermine reason. It's not a rare species.

This possibility of using reason against itself is why the beginning of philosophy is, to use Aristotle's title, "the refutation of sophistry." "Now for some people," Aristotle observed, "it is better worthwhile to seem to be wise, than to be wise without seeming to be (for the art of the sophist is the semblance of wisdom, without the reality); and the sophist is one who makes money from an apparent but unreal wisdom" (165a17–18). Paul, however, prefers sophists to be "demolished," not just "refuted" or exposed as pursuers of money rather than wisdom.

This passage in Paul is mindful of similar advice in 1 Peter (3, 15): "Always be prepared to give an answer to everyone who asks you to give a reason for the hope you have. But do so with gentleness and respect." Paul is more blunt. Some people will not hear if we are overly gentle with them. There is a difference between honest inquirers and sophists.

The last thing many people want to hear today, and somehow

know that they do not dare to hear, is how everything is related to Christ—as it is. What they even less want to hear is that there is a "reason" for every position. How everything is related in Christ is not apart from what is reasonable. Revelation is directed to reason. Reason knows that it does not explain everything. But what completes the explanation is not, in principle, "unreasonable," only beyond, but not against, the powers of finite intellect.

Why Catholicism is being isolated and increasingly persecuted is the nagging suspicion that it can actually give reasons for anything it holds. Even though much of the philosophy of the age is relativism, it cannot afford to deal with reason lest it admit what it denies. Thus Catholicism's calm efforts to state this reasonableness are greeted with shouting, ridicule, avoidance of facts, mis-representation, and hatred. Scripture, to be sure, told us, when invited into a home that refuses to listen, to dust our shoes and move on. But there are increasingly fewer places to where we can move. This fact too seems more and more to focus the attention of the world on the truth issue. This is probably exactly where it needs to be focused.

But it is a world, as I said, that does not much want to listen. In Wodehouse's *The Mating Season*, I read the following passage: "Well, there were these two deaf chaps in the train, don't you know, and it stopped at Wembly, and one of them looked out of the window and said 'This is Wembley', and the other said 'I thought it was Thursday', and the first chap said 'Yes, so am I'." From this rather bemused sketch, we recognize that we often listen but we do not hear what is actually said.

On reading such a passage, I sometimes am tempted to think that a stint in a good English pub would solve most of the world's problems. But where most of the problems seem to occur, such thirst-quenching institutions are generally not allowed. They are considered to be against both reason and religion. That was probably the counter-point of Belloc's "Wherever the Catholic sun doth shine, There's always laughter and good red wine. At least I've always found it so, *Benedicamus Domino*."

To proffer something good about Catholicism in recent decades has been considered, if not impolite, certainly "triumphalistic." Yet,

I wonder if it is not time to face the fact that we are now pretty much left alone with reason and hence revelation addressed to it. We are to state our "reasons" with gentleness and respect, as Peter admonished us. But surely Paul was right. The sophists, usually paid with money, think that they can state any lie or untruth about what we hold as if that is their natural "right." No longer is there much dialogue or debate, only yelling and lies. "Proud pretensions" do raise themselves "against the knowledge of God." In the end, we prefer not merely to "seem to be wise."

Chapter 58

On Merriment

On Saturday, 26 May 1759, Samuel Johnson wrote an untitled essay in *The Idler*. It begins: "Pleasure is very seldom found where it is sought."[1] This reminded me of hearing a joke for the second time, one told by someone else, but one you knew by heart. It is true that you might still laugh, as much humor arises from the way the pleasantry is told, not just the joke itself. But if you know the joke, it cannot be as funny as when you do not know it but "get it" when you did hear it. "He that has anticipated the conversation of a wit, will wonder to what prejudice he owes his reputation," as Johnson later put it.

This "pleasure" passage reminded me of something that Josef Pieper once wrote. "Joy" is always a "by-product." We do not set out to find "joy." We must set out to do what causes joy, namely, what is right, what is true. We even pursue our vices for the good that is in them, distorted as it may be. Joy is a result not a direct object of right choice. It is true that we all prefer to be joyful rather than sad. But it is most likely that, if we set out to be joyful and not rightly to do the work at hand, we will end up sad.

"Our brightest blazes of gladness," Johnson tells us, "are kindled by unexpected sparks." Needless to say, as Schall has a book entitled, *The Classical Moment: Essays on Knowledge and Its Pleasures*, the question can be asked: "Are you not saying that pleasure will come from knowledge and yet be unexpected?"

Aristotle implied that a pleasure is intrinsic to knowing. But it is not the knowing itself. The pleasure only comes indirectly. It only comes when we seek and find the truth of things. It is indeed a

---

1 Samuel Johnson, *Selected Essays* (Harmondsworth: Penguin, 2003), 461–62.

"by-produce." While it is the "truth that makes us free," it is its surprise that makes us glad. The passage from not knowing to knowing is often a long one. But the passage from knowing the truth to being elated by it is instantaneous, again as Aristotle implied.

"Nothing is more hopeless," Johnson continued, "than a scheme of merriment." I recall a phenomenon from somewhere called "organized joy." It meant that something artificial, unfunny, was found when we deliberately, meticulously set out to make everyone laugh. We cringe when we realize that the loud laughter we hear on television is often "canned," often artificially injected. Laugher can indeed be infectious. But we always ask: "But what are they laughing at?"

Yet, is not this very endeavor to cause laughter what the entertainment business thinks it is doing? No doubt it is. And this endeavor is probably why it is closer to "bread and circuses" than it is to merriment, to true joy. C. S. Lewis talked of being "surprised by joy," surprised that reality can fill us with gladness. None the less, we can laugh at what "ain't funny," as Molly McGee used to tell Fibber. The Psalms speak of the Lord laughing to "scorn" those who delight in what is evil.

"Merriment is always the effect of a sudden impression. The jest which is expressed is already destroyed." Humor has to do with seeing the relation in things. But its real source is seeing, at the same time, how our words and ideas could mean something else besides their present contextual meaning. This is why Aristotle thought that our capacity to see the humor of things was a sign of intelligence. For to see the relation of things to each other is also to see how other unexpected relations might also be meant, but, if they were, the whole meaning would be absurd.

The main theme in the latter half of Johnson's short essay on merriment reverts to the implication of intending to be merry. When we set out to do so, we quickly find out, in carrying out our intentions, that all sorts of things go wrong.

A man plans a pleasant journey. Once on his way, however, the road is dusty and the air sultry. He longs for dinner. But the inn he stops at is crowded. His order is "neglected." Finally, he is left to devour "in haste what the cook has spoiled." He looks for a better inn. He finds a more "commodious house" but "the best is always worse than he has expected."

Finally, the man returns to his native city. He expects his old school mates will welcome him and be ready to converse with him. But alas, the first man he looks up barely recognizes his name till he tells him what it is.

"It is seldom that we find either men or places such as we expect them." And this fact is really the best thing that could happen to us. The reality of the person or place we meet or visit is little like the person or place that we expected. If every person and place were exactly as we imagined them to be, we would not need to meet anyone at all. We would already know them. Each man or woman is embodied and en-spirited differently, even while being this man or this woman. This mystery in the other is the beginning of our glory and gladness. We can only be comforted by the realization that we did not create the world.

"Where," we might ask, "are these reflections of Johnson on wit and merriment leading us?" Surprisingly, in following this line of thought, they lead us to hope. "How so?" Here is how Johnson concluded his essay in 1759: "Yet, it is necessary to hope, tho' hope should always be deluded, for hope itself is happiness, and its frustrations, however frequent, are yet less dreadful than its extinction."

That passage is truly remarkable. The loss of hope is the most dreadful thing we can experience as human beings. Thus, "hope itself is happiness." Without it, we are left with "extinction." We are left with our own imagination that thinks it pictures others exactly as they are, but leaves no room for the real person we encounter to enter our souls. Hope implies the laughter and merriment that exist when we see relations we did not anticipate, when we see that the world still makes sense when things go wrong.

We set out to enjoy ourselves and everything goes wrong. Ultimately, we have to laugh at ourselves for ever thinking that our plans "had" to go our way. *Hope is happiness*. It finally means that a better way exists than our way and it keeps breaking into our world. Joy is a "by-product." It arrives when we realize that, in the order of things, the relation of what is right and what is true was intended to surprise us. This surprise, again, is joy, merriment.

"Pleasure is seldom found where it is sought." The conclusion is not that there is no pleasure, but that we often look for it in the wrong places. "Hope is happiness." We cannot but be delighted that nothing that we can concoct by ourselves can really satisfy us, really give us the merriment that does not cease because its source is the surprise that we are not gods.

Chapter 59
On "What Everybody Can Enjoy"

A former student, Nicholas Wheeler, knowing my proclivities, gave me Volume CLXXII of "The World's Classics." The title of this particular volume is: *A Book of English Essays (1600–1900)*. The essays were selected by Stanley V. Makower and Basil H. Blackwell. At the very end of the Preface, we find the following rather touching addendum: "Mr. Makower had not long been engaged on a selection of English essays, when his regretted death left this fruit of his taste and experience in the forming." Basil Blackwell, having finished Merton College, Oxford, went on not only to finish "forming" this volume but also, in 1913, to take over his father's famous book store and publishing business.

The "formed" book was first published in 1912, and reprinted in 1913 (twice) and in 1914. One notes that 1914 was the beginning of the Great War, though I did find a copy of this volume with a 1927 copyright. The publisher was not Blackwell but "Humphrey Milford, Oxford University Press, London Edinburgh Glasgow New York, Toronto Melbourne Bombay." Those were the days when the British still had an empire. It was printed in Oxford by "Horace Hart, Printer to the University."

Mr. Wheeler inscribed, on Candle-mass, 2007, the following explanation of the gift: "I acquired this little collection of essays two years ago when I was in Oxford, and should like you to have it." One can hardly fail to be touched by such a remark, both that a student would think to buy such a book and to know that Schall would particularly enjoy it. The book contains fifty one essays from forty-one authors in 440 pages. The authors include, among others, Hazlitt, Dryden, Sir Richard Steele, Francis Bacon, Francis Thompson, Richard Jeffries, Edgar Allan Poe, and Washington

Irving. Thomas Fuller's "The Good Sea Captain" was particularly good.

Mr. Wheeler next cited three favorite passages from essays in the book. The first was from Sir Thomas Browne, "On Dreams." It read: "That some have never dreamed is as improbable as that some have never laughed." Logically, that remark implies that we all are dreamers and laughers, a comforting thought. Belloc, who was too young to be cited in this book of essays, but who is the language's best essayist, once called us human beings, "we laughers." I have always loved that phrase and was pleased to be reminded of it by none less than Sir Thomas Browne.

The second citation is from Dr. Johnson's "On the Advantages of Living in a Garret." Johnson wrote: "I never think myself qualified to judge a man whom I have only known in one degree of elevation." This means, no doubt, that we must see many levels of a man to know his virtues and, yes, his vices. Even though he clearly knows that we ourselves are not gods, Johnson does not say that we should never judge a man. It is often our responsibility to judge the character, deeds, or veracity of a man. We must decide how he stands to ourselves and others. We are not required to affirm that the acquired character of a man makes no difference in this world. Sometimes it is a life and death matter.

The third passage is from Matthew Arnold's essay, "Dante and Beatrice." It reads: "Dante saw the world, and used in his poetry what he had seen; for he was a born artist. But he was essentially aloof from the world, and not complete in the life of the world; for he was a born spiritualist and solitary." I take this solitariness to mean something of what Cicero meant, citing Cato, that "he was never less alone than when he was alone." In some sense, even to see the world we must at times be alone, be solitary. We must let the world be there; let it happen to us.

I read this essay to which Mr. Wheeler directed my attention. In it, Matthew Arnold was writing about a then recent translation of Dante by Mr. Theodore Martin. Arnold writes: "The *Divine Comedy*...is no allegory, and Beatrice no mere personification of theology. Mr. Martin is quite right in saying that Beatrice is the

Beatrice whom men turned round to gaze at in the streets of Florence." Perhaps no greater wisdom is found than the affirmation that a Beatrice did walk the streets of Florence, a Beatrice who, for Dante, was a "this" Beatrice, who, by the laws of matrimony, was not his.

Arnold's conclusion, however, makes us wonder if he forgot what Dante first saw on the streets of Florence, wonder even if he (Arnold) knew the central doctrine of the Christian faith about our destiny.

> Even to Dante at twenty-one, when he yet sees the living Beatrice with his eyes, she already symbolizes this for him, she is already not the "creature not too bright and good" of Wordsworth, but a spirit far more than a woman; to Dante at twenty-five composing the *Vita Nuova* she is still more a spirit; to Dante at fifty, when his character has taken its bent, when composing his immortal poem, she is a spirit altogether.

No one, not even God, wants for any human Beatrice to be "a spirit far more than a woman." Even Aristotle understood this. Human beings are persons, body and soul, not pure spirits. To love them as pure spirits is not to love them at all. To love them as incarnate persons, we must love them as they are. But loving them as they are always points, necessarily, to that love in which they already exist through no power of their own.

"There is another thought connected with the presence," James Henry Leigh Hunt wrote in his essay in this book, "Shakespeare's Birthday," which "may render the Londoner's walk the more interesting. Shakespeare had neither the vanity which induces a man to be disgusted with *what everybody can enjoy*; nor on the other hand the involuntary self-degradation which renders us incapable of enjoying what is abased by our own familiarity of acquaintanceship." To be "disgusted" with "what everybody can enjoy" is but vanity. Oftentimes, as Chesterton frequently pointed out, we are incapable of enjoying *what is* because we are so used to it that we no longer see its newness and wonder. After all, something we see again and again does not become less wondrous because we see it again and again. This is, in part, what Beatrice herself stood for.

Finally, I note the book's passage from George Eliot's "Authorship." She writes: "It is for art to present images of a lovelier order than the actual; gently winning the affections, and so determining the taste." Recall that the word "taste" was used to describe what the book's editor, before his death, was striving to accomplish in this book. We are "more human," Allan Bloom said, in the Introduction to his *Shakespeare's Politics,* when we are watching a Shakespearean drama than we are in the routine of our daily lives. We see more what we are when we see more clearly what we ought to be, or indeed ought not to be. *Images of a lovelier order than the actual*–the actual order itself is the basis of our wonderment about any "lovelier order."

The "lovelier order" does not take up where the actual order ends. Those who live in the lovelier order are the very ones who lived in the actual order. This is what Beatrice means; otherwise there is only despair. A man should not be "disgusted" with what "everybody can enjoy." The very structure of our being causes us to wonder what it is that "everybody can enjoy." When we filter it all out, this resolution is ultimately what revelation is about.

The good that causes *what is* also is to be, if we choose, our good. This too is what Beatrice on the streets of Florence was about. In this life, however, in our London walks, all of us, like Mr. Makower, remain "in the forming." We seek in our very being images "lovelier" than the present, where, in the same present, there are, indeed, lovely images if we just notice them in spite of the "familiarity of our acquaintanceship." None of the "images" that we ultimately seek had their beginnings elsewhere than in the streets of Florence. When we are told that we are made in the "image and likeness of God," we cannot but be surprised, again to recall Chesterton, that *what is* conforms to what we would want if we could have it.

A "Briefer" Afterword

Books of essays usually do not have conclusions or afterwords. It is not easy to "sum up" a book that touches on everything and nothing and anything. When a reader picks up a book of selected essays, he need not begin with Chapter 1 to work his way, one at a time, through to Chapter 59. Many readers of books like to read the last chapter before they begin it. I am not a fan of this approach, though I have done it myself. Thus, one can begin this book wherever he wants and end it wherever he wants, even at this "A 'Briefer' Afterword."

Yet, as I said in the beginning, the citations at the very start of the book are chosen to put one's mind in the mood for what is to come. When we think of it, what Plato, Aristotle, Johnson, or Wodehouse said, it still provokes us, still brings us to consider the *things that are*. In these pages, we have looked at envy and violence. We have considered why our mind "works" at all in the way it does. And we pondered whether anything more is addressed to us, to our minds, when they are thinking at their best. Is there anything that that we need or would like to listen to? In this sense, to talk of "salvation" and "revelation" makes sense. We need to consider not merely the Whole of finite being, but the origin and meaning of this Whole.

In recent years, I have been particularly struck by an observation that a friend pointed to me in Aquinas, from his *Summa Contra Gentiles*. This is the idea that this universe would not be complete unless there were found in it some being who, from within it, could understand it. The question then becomes, assuming that such a being does exist in the world, as it does: "Can this mind within the universe find out about it?" Is the universe, as I ask in one of the essays, simply "empty"? We still ask: "Why is

there something, not nothing?" If we really think about "nothing," it becomes clear that from it, nothing happens.

These "brief" essays, as I said, are both lightsome and philosophical. We are the beings who, as Aristotle said, can laugh, not only "can" but "do" laugh. This laughter is again the sign of intelligence in us, our capacity to see relations that do or do not fit. As C. S. Lewis put it, we have no "right" to happiness. Most of the essays in this book can be summed up in one overarching thought. If we are ultimately to be happy, to attain "eternal life," and not merely go on and on in "endless duration," it will come to us, not as a "right" or a result of our own enterprise, but as a "gift."

Anything at all that we encounter can cause us to think, yes, can cause merriment. But anything *that is* first comes to us as a gift. Knowing this truth, we can suspect that Gussie Fink-Nottle was right to smile at Bertie Wooster in his perplexity. We began with the problem of "taxing" beer. We now end with "What everyone can enjoy." That seems to be just the right "brief afterword."